Faith That Works

Faith
That
Works

Keswick 2009

Edited by Ali Hull

Authentic

MILTON KEYNES ● COLORADO SPRINGS
● HYDERABAD

Keswick
ministries
bringing the Word alive

15 14 13 12 11 10 09   7 6 5 4 3 2 1

First published 2009 by Authentic Media
9 Holdom Avenue, Bletchley, Milton Keynes, Bucks, MK1 1QR, UK
1820 Jet Stream Drive, Colorado Springs, CO 80921, USA
Medchal Road, Jeedimetla Village, Secunderabad 500 055, A.P., India
www.loveauthentic.com

Authentic Media is a division of Biblica UK, previously IBS-STL UK. Biblica UK
is limited by guarantee, with its registered office at Kingstown Broadway, Carlisle,
Cumbria, CA3 0HA. Registered in England & Wales No. 1216232. Registered
charity in England & Wales No. 270162 and Scotland No. SCO40064

British Library Cataloguing in Publication Data
A catalogue record for this book is available from the
British Library
ISBN 978-1-85078-867-6

Cover design by David Smart
Print Management by Adare
Printed and bound in the UK by J.F. Print Ltd., Sparkford, Somerset

Contents

The Addresses

Introduction by the Chairman of the 2009 Convention

I am delighted that a selection of the teaching given at the 2009 Convention can be made available through this Keswick Year Book. 'Faith that works' was the theme and many commented on the relevance of the subject, and the real help for living that was given through the ministry.

Integrity and reality are always huge issues for the people of God, and certainly in our day when 'spin' in some circles seems to be the accepted 'norm'. We are also assured by many that a person's private life is of no relevance to their public life. Dr Luke, in writing his gospel, gave a report to Theophilus of 'all that Jesus began to DO and to TEACH'. He is the one in whose steps we seek to walk.

Our prayer is that the written record of these sermons will encourage many of us to be diligent in ensuring that 'lip' and 'life' are together in our lives.

Your prayers and support for the Keswick Ministry are deeply appreciated, especially as we prepare for the Convention next year, when the theme will be 'Christ-centred renewal'.

Peter Maiden
September 2009

The Bible Readings

The challenge of living in a fallen world

by Dale Ralph Davis

Dale Ralph Davis

Dale Ralph Davis is a teaching Elder at Woodland Prebyterian Church in Hattiesburg, Mississippi, having previously been a Professor of the Old Testament at the Reformed Theological Seminary, Jackson, Mississippi. He is the author of many books in the 'Focus on the Bible' series, including *Judges, Joshua, 1 and 2 Samuel*, and *1 and 2 Kings*. He is also the author of *The Word Became Fresh: Preaching Old Testament Narratives*. He is married to Barbara and they have three grown-up childen and six grandchildren.

1. The heart that strays: 1 Kings 11

When there is the covenant name of God in the Old Testament text, I usually use 'Yahweh', which is probably as close as we can get to the pronunciation of it. In your text, it is usually written 'The LORD', with Lord in capital letters. I'm used to using Yahweh and, if that is unfamiliar to you, translate it back into 'the LORD'.

Gordon Borror and Ronald Allen tell the story, in their book on worship, of a close friend who had a very painful foot. Walking was increasingly difficult, and so a doctor's help was solicited, X-rays were taken, special shoes were worn, bandages were used – and nothing seemed to give any substantial relief. One day, a mutual friend happened to mention that he had heard of a similar case and suggested that the cause was a bad tooth. No toothache had occurred but a dentist was consulted, X-rays were again taken and a small abscess was found, which had not manifested itself in any local pain as yet. A proper procedure by the dentist brought immediate relief to the foot and it has never hurt since.

Sometimes the trouble is something that is hidden and that is certainly the case in the heart that strays in 1 Kings 11. The world of 1 Kings is a fallen world, and it is important that we see where this fallenness comes from. What does this text demand of us? In its Old Testament form, it is in the words of Joshua 23:11: 'Be very careful, therefore, to love Yahweh your God.' If you prefer the New Testament form, the message is, 'Watch and pray that you may not enter into temptation' (Matt. 26:41).

The arena that matters (vv. 1–4)

> Now King Solomon loved many foreign women, along with the
> daughter of Pharaoh: Moabite, Ammonite, Edomite, Sidonian, and
> Hittite women, from the nations concerning which Yahweh had said
> to the people of Israel, 'You shall not enter into marriage with them,
> neither shall they with you, for surely they will turn away your heart
> after their gods.' Solomon clung to these in love. He had 700 wives,
> princesses, and 300 concubines. And his wives turned away his heart.
> For when Solomon was old his wives turned away his heart after other
> gods, and his heart was not wholly true to Yahweh his God, as was the
> heart of David his father.

What is the problem here? You will notice, when you get into
1 Kings 11, that there is a big contrast with what went before. It is
very different – everything seems to fall apart in chapter 11.
Certain scholars say that they see hidden difficulties under the text
in chapters 1 to 10 but it's a very positive picture overall. The kingdom is established and Israel is happy (chapters 1 to 4), you have
the building of the temple and establishing of temple worship
(chapters 5 to 8) and in chapter 10 you have worldwide recogni-
tion of Solomon. Then you get to chapter 11 and what a contrast!
Let me just quote from one writer with whom I agree entirely:
'Some writers moan so much over what they divine of Solomon's
affluence, indulgence, excesses, extravagance, exploitation and
oppression, that one could be duped into thinking that such items
are the principal trouble.' Chapter 11 clearly trumpets that the
problem is not wealth, luxury, high-handedness, wisdom, popular-
ity, renown, splendour or achievement but other gods. Solomon
went after other gods.

What is the deeper problem than other gods? Notice a very key
verb (vv. 1,2): 'Solomon loved many foreign women'. It is a matter of
love. That same verb is used in 1 Kings 3:3 at the beginning of
Solomon's reign: 'Solomon loved Yahweh, walking in the statutes of
David his father'. The deeper problem has to do with an emotional
attachment.

Probably you have noticed how difficult it is to deal with professing Christians who are taken with a certain pattern of action. They may be wanting to step out on their spouse and take up with someone else and they have their own rationale for that. It is an emotional attachment and it is very difficult to bring to bear scriptural, rational and logical arguments. They are going to go on anyway because they have a commitment to that path of action and then you pick up the pieces afterwards.

The real problem with Solomon was his heart. In the text here, the word 'heart' is noted four times. The wives were 'from the nations concerning which Yahweh had said to the people of Israel, "You shall not enter into marriage with them, neither shall they with you, for surely they will turn away your *heart* after their gods." . . . For when Solomon was old his wives turned away his *heart* after other gods, and his *heart* was not wholly true to Yahweh his God, as was the *heart* of David his father.' (my italics) His concern, back in 1 Kings 3:9,12, when God asks him what he wants him to give him, was his heart. Solomon says, literally, 'So give your servant a discerning heart to govern your people and to distinguish between right and wrong.' But now he doesn't have a listening heart, he has a divided heart. It has turned aside after other gods. It is a heart problem.

We need to touch on this a little bit, because the way our culture deals with the heart is to limit it to the emotions. There was a movie, maybe ten years ago, in the States, in which the defending attorney was making his final statement to the jury in the courtroom and he said to them, 'Don't make your decision based on what's here with your mind' – based on what your mind tells you to do: 'do it on the basis of your emotions, your feelings.' That is a scary thing to do in a court of law.

There is a danger that you can have too much emphasis in an academic institution on academics, but I never did think we packed enough into the heads and minds of the students, who were usually quite willing to slack off in the academic area anyway. Nevertheless we used to have people come to the seminary where I used to teach, speaking in chapel, and every once in a while for some reason they might make the point that it is not what is up here in your head that matters, it is what is in your heart. While I get the point and understand their concerns, I do not like the divorce between head and heart. I think in the Bible the head is in the heart or the heart is in the head and I don't care which way you want to put it, but they seem to be together. In Mark 7:21–23, Jesus says, 'For from within, out of the heart of man, come evil thoughts, sexual immorality, theft, murder, adultery, coveting, wickedness, deceit, sensuality, envy, slander, pride, foolishness. All these evil things come from within, and they defile a person.' In American and English culture, the heart is mainly emotion and feeling, but in the Scripture the heart is the willing, feeling, thinking centre of a person.

What's so haunting about the internal condition of Solomon here is that his very last recorded spoken words, in Scripture, are 1 Kings 8 where he says to Israel that they should be careful to make sure their hearts were wholly with Yahweh, their God. The same language is used in verse 4 where it says that Solomon's heart was *not* completely with Yahweh his God. What a haunting irony that is.

This is the arena that matters – what we cannot see. About seven years ago, there was a house near the border between the United States and Mexico, about seventy miles east of San Diego, California. US drug agents broke into the house and then into a closet in the house. They found an entrance to a 1,200 foot tunnel, complete with electric lights, ventilation ducts and wooden walls. It ended in a fireplace in a house just beyond the metal wall that separates the United States from Mexico. It was the conduit for a lucrative drug-smuggling regime that smuggled billions of dollars of cocaine, marijuana and other drugs into the States. But it just looked like a normal house. That is the arena that matters: what you can't see, deep underneath. The Old Testament warns you of this internal problem. So you ask yourself, 'If this is the arena that matters, is there a drift in my preferences that's going on now, that no one else can see because it's from within?'

The age that matters (vv. 4–8)

Verse 4 tells us that Solomon's wives had turned away his heart when he became old. It was a process that was going on, a gradual thing. It took time to develop and then it became visible: 'For Solomon went after Ashtoreth the goddess of the Sidonians, and after Milcom the abomination of the Ammonites. . . . Then Solomon built a high place for Chemosh the abomination of Moab, and for Molech the abomination of the Ammonites, on the mountain east of Jerusalem. And so he did for all his foreign wives, who made offerings and sacrificed to their gods' (1 Kgs. 11:5,7,8).

It wasn't just something that remained behind closed doors. It showed itself visibly: what is in the heart usually does come out in the open. Notice when this occurred: at the time of Solomon's old age. It was a gradual process but it was complete by then. Sometimes we don't realize what a dangerous age our mature years are. We tend to think that when we retire, 'Maybe I can just go on autopilot. I can let down a little and coast, can't I?' I don't think so.

In Genesis 12:1, Yahweh says to Abram: 'Go from your country and your kindred and your father's house to the land that I will show you.' Who knows what a crisis that must have been in Abraham's approximately seventy-fifth year? He was told to separate himself from everything that was near and dear . . . Then to have that promise given to him, that impossible promise, 'To your offspring I will give this land' and he couldn't have any offspring. Hanging over from Genesis 11:30 are the words, 'Now Sarai was barren; she had no child.' Finally, you get to chapter 21 and Isaac is born miraculously, and you say, 'I can rest a bit.' Then Genesis 22:2 comes and Yahweh says to Abraham, 'Take your son, your only son Isaac, whom you love, and go to the land of Moriah, and offer him there as a burnt offering on one of the mountains of which I shall tell you.'

Abraham is in his mature years, and sometimes it is in our latter years that we face our biggest tests. Many of you have faced tragedies and distresses that have nearly crushed you early on in your life, but there are many of us who have not yet faced what we would call an overwhelming tragedy. I think churches and ministers need to be aware of this. We tend to think, if we have people that are 60 and over, you just talk a little bit louder to them, you humour them along and you collect the tithe from their retirement cheques. And if they don't make much trouble, you hope they're very happy. But think about it. Normally those people are going to be facing their biggest trials in life, if they haven't faced them already: loss of health; loss of a spouse; loneliness; cancer and death. They need the ministry of God's people to them. Don't throw money at it and don't think you have to hire a minister for seniors: just give them prayer and care, but see how critical this age is. We can never let down in being concerned with our heart faithfulness to Jesus; it's the age that matters.

Back to this point just once more. Did you notice it was gradual? Solomon did not get blown away with paganism. He got worn down with it. It was a matter of ongoing wear.

When we were living in Jackson, Mississippi, we had a basketball goal in the backyard, attached to a tree. The backboard was made out of pressed board: we call it particle board, and in a climate like Mississippi where there's a lot of moisture and heat, over time that wears away. We didn't notice, we just played basketball. One day, we were shooting around and my brother-in-law threw up a shot and hit the backboard. The whole side of that backboard came out over the bolt and dropped down. We hadn't noticed it, but as the moisture worked around the bolt, it expanded and destroyed the backboard. But it was imperceptible to us. That's what can be the case. You may not find out until years later when it becomes obvious that your heart has gone astray. Your senior years are the age that matters; don't go from being a faithful disciple to being an old fool.

The anger that matters (vv. 9,10)

Yahweh 'was angry with Solomon, because his heart had turned away from Yahweh, the God of Israel, who had appeared to him twice and had commanded him concerning this thing, that he should not go after other gods. But he did not keep what Yahweh commanded.' Have you ever noticed how the God of the Bible has never been able to get into pluralism? He just doesn't fit our times or our mentality. Why should he be so irate if someone wants to spread their devotion around? Solomon was just wanting to broaden himself by investigating alternative forms of spirituality.

Those of us who have the privilege to live in quasi-democracies are used to a certain freedom of religious expression. Governments maybe don't always do it as well as we like, but they seek to guarantee a certain freedom in this area. So if someone wants to worship a bowl of roasted peanuts, they can: they've got a civil right to do that. But that doesn't mean that Yahweh will approve of it. He will judge us for that. Here you have a strange God, because Yahweh is the only God like that. He's the only deity in the ancient Near East who required exclusive devotion. In pagan theology, gods and goddesses didn't get upset if you wanted to worship another god or pray to a multiplicity of other deities, but Yahweh isn't that way. Which is one reason I worship Yahweh, because he's the only God that's a jealous God. There is no one else like him.

President Lyndon Johnson in the US used to tell of a story that took place during the Depression in the 1930s. Times were hard and there was a young man who was desperate for a teaching job. He appeared before a school board, in the Texas hill country, applying for a position. The board was very impressed: the man was eloquent, well informed, articulate and conscientious. So when the interview ended, they said to him, 'We think we would like to have you teach here but there's one thing we have to ask you. We have some difference of opinion in our community about geography and we want to know which side you're on. Do you teach that the world is round or do you teach that the world is flat?' And the young man immediately said, 'I can teach it either way.'

That's what we want but that's not what Yahweh is. He's this strange, jealous God who demands exclusive devotion. And isn't it true that that's the way the Lord Jesus is, in Matthew 10:37,38? 'Whoever loves father or mother more than me is not worthy of me, and whoever loves son or daughter more than me is not worthy of me. And whoever does not take his cross and follow me is not worthy of me.' What's he saying? He's saying, 'I must have the place of supreme devotion in your life.' What is that but a reassertion of the first commandment? Who does Jesus think he is? That's our God. No wonder he is angry when we two-time him with other gods, as Solomon did.

Notice the aggravation of God's anger in verse 9. Yahweh is angry with Solomon 'because his heart had turned away from Yahweh, the God of Israel, who had appeared to him twice.' This refers to 1 Kings 3:4–15, where Yahweh appeared to Solomon in a dream and said, 'Ask what I shall give you.' That's when Solomon asked for a listening heart. Then, after the temple was dedicated, Yahweh appeared to Solomon again. The emphasis there is more on warning: 'You must continue and Israel must continue to be faithful to me or I will make this house a heap of ruins.'

Twice Yahweh had appeared to Solomon. Think of the condescension, the kindness, the explicitness, the clarity that God bent over backwards to give to Solomon. What gracious goodness he showed on these two occasions. Do you see the inference we have to make from this? The most privileged, intimate, ecstatic experiences with God do not guarantee immunity from unfaithfulness. It's scary. The implication is that you can speak in tongues, you can have superb and rich devotional times and you can end up salivating after other gods and being under the anger of the God you have shunned.

The anchor that matters (vv. 11–13)

Therefore Yahweh said to Solomon, 'Since this has been your practice and you have not kept my covenant and my statutes that I have commanded you, I will surely tear the kingdom from you and will give it to your servant. Yet for the sake of David your father I will not do it in your days, but I will tear it out of the hand of your son. However, I will not tear away all the kingdom, but I will give one tribe to your son, for the sake of David my servant and for the sake of Jerusalem that I have chosen.'

It doesn't say where this word came from. It may have come through a prophet. It doesn't say and it doesn't matter. What matters is what the Lord said here. Notice that what the Lord is saying to Solomon in verse 11 is that he's going to have a kind of Saul experience: 'I will surely tear the kingdom from you'. That conjures up memories of 1 Samuel 15:27,28 where, as Samuel was turning to go, after Saul had been rejected as king of Israel, Saul grabbed Samuel's robe and it tore. Samuel said, 'Yahweh has torn the kingdom of Israel from you . . .' Now it's going to be torn away from Solomon – and yet with a limitation. Notice what verses 12 and 13 say; he's going to tear the kingdom from Solomon but not now and not all the kingdom. There are certain non-negotiables here. Notice he says, 'I won't do it in your days because of David your father.' There is a similar reason in verse 13: 'for the sake of David my servant'. It could mean because of the fidelity of David that he showed to Yahweh. It was not perfect fidelity, but it was clearly consistent: that could be part of it, for David did show that. But it may mean more. When he says, 'for the sake of David your father' it could and probably does mean, 'for the sake of the promise I made to David your father'.

There was a covenant with David from 2 Samuel 7:12–16. The Lord had said that if one of his descendants was unfaithful, he would discipline him and judge him (and there were going to be rascals and reprobates in David's line of kings) and they would be judged accordingly, but they weren't going to short-circuit God's kingdom plan. As he said, he would establish David's line of kings, he would establish his throne, and even though later Israel and Judah went through the Exile, that Davidic line of kings sprouted again in Matthew 1:1–17 and consummated in Jesus, the Messiah, from David's line. Essentially what the Lord is telling Solomon here is, 'I'm going to judge you but the judgement on you and Israel is not going to be total, because I've made certain previous commitments. My judgement takes place within the orbit of my promises, and my judgements will never nullify my promises.'

Notice the two-pronged element of promise: 'I'll give to him one tribe because of David my servant and because of Jerusalem, which I had chosen.' David is the king. Jerusalem has the temple: the orthodox proper worship of God. David is the royal person. Jerusalem is the atoning place, where the sacrifices of atonement were made for the sins of God's people. So you have those two prongs: royal person and atoning place. And how are those fulfilled, when you run on down the timeline of history and into the New Testament era? They are fulfilled in the royal person, Jesus the Son of David, who will reign on David's throne, and they are fulfilled in the place of the cross, outside Jerusalem (cf. Heb. 13). That is the place where atonement is made for God's people and their sins. The thrust of this is, here is an anchor. The promises that God has made, regarding the royal person and the atoning place, are going to come to pass, though he judges Solomon and Israel for their unfaithfulness. There are some things that simply cannot undo that. It will come to pass.

In our war in the United States back in the 1860s, there was a fellow by the name of Daniel Adams, who was practising law in Louisiana when the war broke out. So he accepted a commission in the First Louisiana Regulars as a lieutenant-colonel. Now at the battle of Shiloh in western Tennessee, just north of the Mississippi border, the general of those Louisiana Regulars was hit with a cannonball and killed and so Daniel Adams had to take over command. Later that same day, Adams was struck in the head by a musket ball as well, and the musket ball went in above his left eye and came out behind his left ear. Obviously he was helpless and insensible and so he was taken to a field hospital and then later thrown onto a wagon that was transporting wounded men down to Mississippi for further treatment. The driver of the wagon on which Adams' body was piled didn't see any signs of life in him, and was having trouble making headway on a muddy road, and so he took Adams' body and threw it off to the side of the road. There he would have died, except there were some fellows from the Tenth Mississippi who came marching by in the retreat. They happened to notice some signs of life and hurried Adams to a nearby hospital. Now in the war between the states, going to a hospital was not necessarily good news. But in any case, they got him there and, incredibly, Adams survived his injuries and was promoted to brigadier-general, and four months later he was pronounced fit for duty.

What's so amazing about that? Well, if you had a hole through above your left eye and behind your left ear and it was 1862, you would probably be *kaput*. But somehow Daniel Adams refused to die. That's what you have with Yahweh's promises. There are certain things Yahweh sets out to do and he's going to do them. And your sin doesn't have the power to overthrow that promise. It doesn't excuse your unfaithfulness and it doesn't excuse Israel's. We can bring immense shame to Christ's name, we can bring huge misery to ourselves and others by our sin and rebellion and by our divided hearts, but we don't have the power to overthrow God's promised kingdom plan. He will bring his royal person of David's line, who will reign, and he will bring the atoning sacrifice in Jerusalem, and you can't stop that. Isn't it good news to have this anchor? David's throne is occupied, and that Jerusalem blood does cleanse us from all our sin. And that person and that place, that work, you cannot undo. Already in 1 Kings 11 is a defective son of David. You will have to wait for another son of David who will look at all the kingdoms of the world and their glory (Matt. 4:8) and whose heart will *not* turn aside from Yahweh his God. And you must take care that you do not forsake your first love.

2. Facing self-styled religion: 1 Kings 13

Introduction

Charles Colson, in one of his books, has passed on something that was in Robert Bellah's book called *Habits of the Heart*, in which he interviewed a young lady by the name of Sheila. Sheila said, 'I believe in God. I can't remember the last time I went to church, but my faith has carried me a long way. It's Sheilaism, just my own little voice.'[1] Then in one of Michael Horton's books, he quotes an article that was entitled 'Supper for one', in which the writer advocates supplementing private devotions with a private communion service with water or juice and crackers.

You have that, only on a larger scale, in 1 Kings 12 and 13, when we come to the reign of Jeroboam in the northern kingdom of Israel – it was the same in principle under Jeroboam. The kingdom split, after Solomon. The southern kingdom, Judah, was with Rehoboam, and Jeroboam became king of the ten northern tribes we call Israel. That was about 931BC and Jeroboam had decided that he needed to institute a new fashion in worship (1 Kgs. 12:25–33).

Jeroboam began to think, and he was driven by fear (1 Kgs. 12:26,27). He figured, 'If the people still go up to the southern kingdom to worship, they're still going up to Jerusalem to the temple and their hearts are going to be turned back. They're going to find their loyalty again to Rehoboam and to the line of David's kings. Then they will come back and kill me, and it will all be over. So in order to secure myself, I need to use some of my savvy.' So he decided to institute his own brand of worship, his Jeroboamism, you might say. It was driven by subjectivism.

He set up these two bull calf shrines, one in Dan in the north, one in Bethel in the south of his kingdom. Notice it says (1 Kgs. 12:33) that the feast that he held in the eighth month 'he had devised from his own heart'. The writer has his own subtle way of insisting that this was Jeroboam's own thing; he uses the very common word 'made'. It is a very common Hebrew verb and you see it repeatedly in chapter 12. In verse 28, 'the king . . . made two calves of gold.' In verse 31, 'he also made temples on high places and appointed' – in other words, 'made' – 'priests from among all the people'. In verse 32, he made a feast, that's the same verb, though it's translated differently. He made, he made, he made, he did it! I think the writer is mocking Jeroboam: 'This is his concoction, this is what he made.'

So there you have it, Jeroboam's new scheme. Notice that Jeroboam did not say that the worship in Jerusalem, orthodoxy, was not true. He said it was too dangerous. And so he set up his own shrines and he said to Israel (1 Kgs. 12:28), 'You have gone up to Jerusalem long enough.' In other words, 'We're going to have our own worship right here in the north.'

Some scholars have this idea that what Jeroboam did was not all that deviant: some even make him out to be a reformer. I don't want to go into that, but suffice it to say that, far from being just a mild affair, Ahijah the prophet (1 Kgs. 14:9) said, 'you have . . . made for yourself other gods'. Those bull images were other gods, and the sad thing about it was that Jeroboam was the very first king of the northern kingdom and yet, according to 1 and 2 Kings, the beginning was the beginning of the end. You can see that, in Ahijah the prophet's own words (1 Kgs. 14:6–16). At the very beginning of the northern kingdom, Jeroboam had delivered a lethal injection into the bloodstream of Israel, and it never ceased to affect them and lead them to destruction.

So you have a new crisis here, and chapter 13 continues the story. Ignore the chapter division: chapter 13 takes up the bullish dedication

service that is going on in Bethel as they dedicate the shrine. Notice
that this strange story focuses on the theme of the word of God. As
you read through it, you'll see repeatedly the phrase, 'the word of
Yahweh' or 'the word of the LORD' or 'the word that the LORD spoke'.
Sometimes it'll be described a little differently, 'what the LORD had
commanded' or something like that, but the word of Yahweh, the
word of the Lord, occurs some ten or eleven times throughout the
chapter. The theme is the word of God. That's suggestive: it tells us
what we need to focus on. Here's the point: what matters is not so
much how you face the latest religious crisis. We're always in a crisis,
aren't we? There's always some sort of crisis in the church. What matters is not so much how you face the latest religious crisis, where there
will always be one, but how you deal with the word of God already
available to you.

Perversity in the face of clarity (vv. 1–6, 33, 34)

As we try to unpack the teaching of chapter 13, and understand the
narrative at least basically, I'd like to pick up each of the key characters and try to characterize them in relation to the word of God.

First of all, we have King Jeroboam. It is a quite an interruption for
a formal church service (1 Kgs. 13:1,2). Here you have the dedication
of the Bethel campus, and all of a sudden, out of nowhere, a man of
God from Judah, the southern kingdom, comes barging in. He looks
at the altar and begins preaching at it. 'O altar, altar, thus says Yahweh:
"Behold, a son shall be born to the house of David, Josiah by name,
and he shall sacrifice on you the priests of the high places who make
offerings on you, and human bones shall be burned on you"' (v. 2).
Then he gave a sign (v. 3): 'the altar shall be torn down, and the ashes
that are on it shall be poured out.' It was quite an interruption but an
apostasy doesn't deserve manners.

You might say there was a double or triple sign. There was one sign
of power (v. 4): Jeroboam stretched out his hand and said, 'Grab that
guy!' Then he couldn't get his hand back, it was frozen. Then there
was a sign of truth (v. 5): the altar *was* torn down. It was split apart and

'the ashes poured out from the altar, according to the sign that the man of God had given'. So that authenticated his word in verse 2, in which he predicted the future, about a king who would come, Josiah, a Davidic king. He would wreck this worship. The word is for the future but the sign is in the present, and when the sign actually comes to pass in the present, it shows that that future word is guaranteed and sure.

So there was a sign of power on Jeroboam's hand and arm; there was a sign of truth in the splitting of the altar and then there was a sign of grace as well. The king begins to eat humble pie (v. 6) and he asked the fellow to intercede for him that his hand might be restored. He did and it was. It was a sign of grace. That's enough to convince everybody. You have these signs authenticating that word and yet what do you have overall? Though Jeroboam had all this evidence, you find perversity in the face of clarity. Verses 33 and 34 tell you this final response: 'After this thing Jeroboam did not turn from his evil way, but made priests for the high places again from among all the people. Any who would, he ordained to be priests of the high places. And this thing became sin to the house of Jeroboam'. Did it change one thing for Jeroboam?

Now you might say, 'That man of God from Judah was disobedient and lost his life. It may have been that that made Jeroboam think that he didn't have to pay attention to him.' I tend to think that it would mean all the more that he would have to pay attention, because the man of God from Judah had told Jeroboam he wasn't allowed to eat bread or drink water there. If Jeroboam had found out that he had lost his life and had stayed behind in Israel, it would only show that the word of Yahweh was still true. I don't think we can get around that.

The problem is that we assume that if you are clear, people will get it. About a year ago, in our paper, there was an Andy Capp cartoon; Andy and his wife have just come from seeing the marriage counsellor. His wife says, 'That was so funny!' Andy is laughing and then his wife quotes the marriage counsellor: 'Perhaps you could try conversing with each other in the evening.' Then she chuckles about that. Andy says, 'Yeah, I know, like we don't have a TV!' You think you're getting through but they just don't get it.

That's the way it is with Jeroboam. You can make this false assumption that people cannot ignore clear evidence, but they do. Ask Joe Stalin. Back in 1941, all the evidence pointed to the fact that Hitler was going to be attacking the Soviet Union, even though they had this pact. Everybody tried to warn Stalin of a Nazi attack. Churchill sent him specific information, confirmed by the American embassy. There was a Soviet spy in Tokyo and he produced details of the German invasion plan of the Soviet Union and its correct date; Stalin also had circumstantial warnings from his generals, but he let it be known that he didn't want to hear about it. So, as Paul Johnson says, 'Stalin, who trusted nobody else, appears to have been the last human being on earth to trust Hitler's words.' He had evidence upon evidence, all kinds of warning and it didn't get through.

In 1 Kings 18, you have the same thing working. The priests of Baal cry all day and they can't get Baal to burn up the sacrifice with fire. Then Elijah prays and Yahweh responds and sends fire from heaven. You can imagine what happens when Ahab goes home to Jezebel and tells her about what happened. He says something like this: 'Jezebel, honey,' (he was the only one who ever called Jezebel 'honey') 'you should have seen it. The Baal prophets couldn't do anything. Nothing came. Then Elijah just repaired this altar and he put the sacrifice there and he had it sopping wet. There was water around in the trench and he simply prayed earnestly to Yahweh, and he sent fire. It slurped up everything, even the water in the trench and you should have seen it.' You can see Jezebel turning away from her mirror, levelling her narrow mascara-laden eyes with a look of scorn at Ahab and saying, with Revlon-curled lips, 'So?'

There's the problem. You can have clear evidence – it can be as clear as Carmel – and people will refuse to get it. It's perversity in the face of clarity. We have a bunch of little Jeroboams still running around in the church. What about the one who says, 'I know what the Bible says about marrying only in the Lord, but . . .' What about the one who says, 'I know that text in Hebrews, about not forsaking the assembling of ourselves together, but I'm in a non-church mode right now.' Or, 'I know what the Bible says and what Jesus says about being eager to reconcile with my brother who has something against me, but . . .' It's not that the Bible is unclear, it's that we're perverse.

Folly in the face of sufficiency (vv. 11–24)

Jeroboam was ever the suave politician and, after his hand was restored, he invited the man of God from Judah home for lunch – only to be rebuffed. He suggested he could cut him a cheque perhaps for his expenses or something like that but no, he was rebuffed. Yahweh, the man of God from Judah said, had given his servant a clear word (1 Kgs. 13:8–10): 'I will not eat bread or drink water in this place, for so was it commanded me by the word of Yahweh, saying, "You shall neither eat bread nor drink water nor return by the way that you came." So he went another way and did not return by the way that he came to Bethel.'

He went away lunchless, and so far so good. But then (v. 11 onwards) there were a couple of sons of an old prophet in the northern kingdom. We don't know any more background on him. They go home and tell their dad what a strange thing happened that day. The old prophet wanted to know which way the man of God from Judah went, and he came upon the man, sitting under a tree, perhaps taking a break (v. 14). Bethel is only something like six miles from the border of Judah. I don't know why he had to take any extended rest there, but he did. The old prophet asked the man of God from Judah to lunch, and the man of God reiterated the same reply he'd given to Jeroboam, the clear word he had from Yahweh against any table fellowship north of the border (vv. 16,17). Then comes the counter revelation claim of verse 18. The old prophet says, 'I also am a prophet as you are, and an angel spoke to me by the word of Yahweh, saying, "Bring him back with you into your house that he may eat bread and drink water." But he lied to him.'

The last two words in the Hebrew text of verse 18 are so abrupt. It's translated, 'But he lied to him' – it's just two Hebrew words, and there's no 'but' in the Hebrew. The translators have supplied that; at the end of verse 18, it's simply that phrase. Not a 'but' nor a 'however' but rather just a dash at the end – he lied to him.

What baffles me is that the man of God from Judah went with him (v. 19), without apparently expressing any scepticism, without asking any questions, without demanding any proof. Why did he do that? I don't know. The writer isn't trying to answer all our questions. But how do you argue with people in this day and age, who say 'The Lord said to me'? I hope you take that with more than one grain of salt. Sometimes they're just speaking loosely. They may mean something like, 'The Lord is impressing on me to say' or 'The Lord is impressing on me to do such a thing.' Or they might be saying, 'The Lord is giving me a nudge about this.' They might express it that way: 'The Lord said to me.' It's very hard to contradict, but you ought to be sceptical about it.

There was once a fellow in my father's first pastorate that went over to another man's farm. He felt that he needed to talk to this man about his soul, and he knocked on the door. The wife answered and the fellow asked if her husband was home. She said no, he wasn't. He said, 'The Holy Spirit told me to come over and talk to your husband.' So the wife said, 'If the Holy Spirit had told you to come over and talk to my husband, the Holy Spirit would have made sure my husband was at home.'

It's very easy to claim 'The Lord said to me.' But this old prophet claimed it, and the guy went home with him. Then, while they munched lunch, the old prophet had a real word from Yahweh for him (vv. 20–22). That's the guy who lied! Yes, but he is also one through whom the true word of God can come

> And he cried to the man of God who came from Judah, 'Thus says Yahweh, "Because you have disobeyed the word of Yahweh and have not kept the command that Yahweh your God commanded you, but have come back and have eaten bread and drunk water in the place of which he said to you, 'Eat no bread and drink no water,' your body shall not come to the tomb of your fathers."'

And so it turned out. The old preacher lets him take his donkey but a lion meets and kills him, and then the lion decides he's not hungry for either preacher or donkey. This is clearly supernatural. Notice in verses 24, 25 and 28, it says the lion was standing beside the body. Here's a lion that kills a man and doesn't maul or consume him. I don't know what that old prophet did when he went back, if the lion was still there. What do you say, 'Run along now'? But that was meant to impress on us that's there's something more than what's merely human and ordinary going on here.

The old prophet, who lied and then who spoke a true word from the Lord, insisted that the prophecy of the man of God from Judah would prove true (v. 32), even if that man of God from Judah had not remained true to the word given him about eating and drinking in Bethel.

Lots of questions come up as you read this passage. Why was he taking a rest under the tree (v. 14) if by implication haste was required? Why did he go with the lying prophet? Why did the liar lie? Why did the man of God from Judah not at least protest? But don't let all this strangeness and all your curious questions crowd out what's clear – which is that the man of God from Judah had what he needed: he had Yahweh's clear word. Why do we think we need more? 'More' may be the mantra of the discontented evangelical church in our day. Yahweh has breathed out the sacred writings 'that the man of God may be competent, equipped for every good work' (2 Tim. 3:17). We don't really believe that. We want something more: more sensational than the word, something more attention-grabbing, more titillating than the mere word of God. The man of God from Judah needed nothing else for obedience but he fell for the revelation claim of another, for someone who pretended to have more. But if you have received the word of Yahweh, as it's wrapped up in Scripture, and you have a conviction about the full sufficiency of Scripture, it ought to lead you to have a settled contentment with Scripture.

We drag ourselves to conferences and we latch on to gimmicks and we go to seminars and we visit websites and we read the blogs of the current church gurus and we institute special programmes and we add supplementary ministries. We do everything to jazz up church. But we have the word. We just don't think it's enough. Jesus has given his church the word and the sacraments and we're saying, in essence, by our practice, 'We want more.'

Duplicity in the face of certainty (vv. 18–32)

What made this fellow tick, this old prophet from Bethel? We have an eccentric prophet here. And we wonder why the man of God from Judah was dawdling (v. 14) – perhaps there was some deficiency in him. But the real problem is in verse 18. The old prophet from Bethel tried to deliberately ruin the man of God from Judah. Why? Perhaps the old prophet wasn't as against the new measures of Jeroboam as the man of God from Judah was. Perhaps he wasn't willing to stand up against Jeroboam but he was willing to wreck someone who did. Perhaps that's why God brought someone from Judah, because there were no willing servants in Israel. We can only observe what's here; we can't imagine what's not.

The old prophet lied to the servant of God and this is the irony. He is the liar (v. 18) who speaks the truth (vv. 20–22). He lied to the servant of God and yet he affirmed the truth of his word, and especially the word that the man of God from Judah had spoken about the future (v. 32). This weird prophet was himself the channel of God's true word, at least at lunchtime that day. What I want you to see is that this old prophet from Bethel sports an alarming combination: he speaks the truth of God, he believes the word of God – and he destroys the servant of God. If we want to put this into technical lingo, I suppose we could say what you have here is orthodoxy without sanctification. It's dangerous. Jesus said there would be folks like this (Matt. 7:21–23)

> Not everyone who says to me, 'Lord, Lord,' will enter the kingdom of heaven, but the one who does the will of my Father who is in heaven. On that day many will say to me, 'Lord, Lord, did we not prophesy in your name, and cast out demons in your name, and do many mighty works in your name?' And then will I declare to them, 'I never knew you; depart from me, you workers of lawlessness.'

It's possible to have the word, to know the word, but not to embrace the word. That seems to be where this old prophet from Bethel was. It's possible to have orthodoxy and not have holiness, you might say.

You might be a professional disciple but not a genuine disciple. He had the word, he knew the word, he could speak the word, but the word didn't have him. There was a certain detachment about it.

I found a sort of confession in Iain Murray's biography of Martyn Lloyd-Jones.[2] He passes on a letter that one of Lloyd-Jones' former medical associates wrote to him, after Lloyd-Jones had had surgery. He was telling Lloyd-Jones to please not try to go back to his work too quickly, to take time to recover. In that letter, the doctor said this: 'Having seen well over seventy thousand operations in fifty years, I'm ashamed to say that I rather looked upon them as more or less normal incidents in life. I then had three major abdominal operations in three consecutive years. And I discovered the difference between watching the proceedings from a stool and being the patient on the table.' We can have a professional, detached way of looking at things, and we can be in the midst of it, where it lays hold of us. This old prophet had had the word, knew the word, could speak the word, but the word really didn't claim him. He was willing to ruin a messenger of the word.

Jesus said that many will commend their ministries of pulpit and power at the last day – the ones whom he will address as those working lawlessness. You should be terrified if you have the truth and yet that truth does not grip, control and transform you.

Our problem, then, is not how are we going to face the next Jeroboam crisis, but rather, how are we holding to the word we've already been given?

3. Living under anti-Christ's regime: 1 Kings 16:29 – 17:16

Introduction

In September 1698, Peter the Great returned to Russia. I don't know if that was immediately after his western tour, but all his lackeys came to welcome him. They were all gathered round and he was receiving them with pleasure – and he produced a long sharp barber's razor and proceeded to cut off all their beards. There were several who were spared but these people, who'd had lips and chins and cheeks covered up with beards for any number of years, had them exposed. It was a cultural thing and it was quite a shock. But Peter thought that this made his people an object of mirth and mockery in the west and he was determined to end it. It was a visible symbol that he meant to impose, a sign of the change that was coming in Russia: a seismic shift.

There was a seismic shift that came in the northern kingdom of Israel about 874BC to 852BC under the reign of Ahab, son of Omri. Had they known the New Testament, maybe they would have thought that anti-Christ had arrived ahead of schedule in Ahab's regime. As the church today also lives in shaky times and dark days, I think we need the testimony of this text.

The days are evil (1 Kgs. 16:29–34)

What was so unique about this time in Israel under Ahab's regime? On the surface it wasn't bad. There was stability. Ahab reigned for twenty-two years (v. 29): that was pretty good because, if you read back preceding this section, you'll find that there was quite a turnover in rulers in Israel. Finally, someone actually reigns for a period of years: and there was prosperity as well. Ahab married Jezebel the daughter of Ethbaal, king of the Sidonians (v. 31): this marital partnership between Israel and Phoenicia and Sidon would open up a port. Israelite products could go out: so it was probably a sign of prosperity for Israel. But there was a darker side (vv. 30,33): 'Ahab . . . did evil in the sight of Yahweh, more than all who were before him . . . Ahab did more to provoke Yahweh, the God of Israel, to anger than all the kings of Israel who were before him.' But exactly what was unique about Ahab's time?

A unique pressure

It seems that Ahab had some enthusiasm for Jezebel's Baal worship (v. 31): he 'served Baal and worshipped him'; (v. 32), 'He erected an altar for Baal in the house of Baal, which he built in Samaria.' It seems maybe Ahab had a conversion of some sort. The problem with Jezebel was that, for her, Baalism was no private faith. She followed worldview Baalism: she had her own Baal groupies, subsidized by the government (1 Kgs. 18:19); she was the one who wore the pants in the kingdom (1 Kgs. 21:25); she was butchering Yahweh's prophets (1 Kgs. 18:4,13); she was the one who would squash those who remained loyal to Yahweh (1 Kgs. 21:4–15). She was the one who may have been behind the ripping down of Yahweh's altars and worship centres in the northern kingdom (1 Kgs. 18:30; 19:10,14). Jezebel was a soul winner for Baal, and she was all the more effective because, in a lot of ways, she *was* the government.

A unique lure

Baal worship traded in fertility, and this involve both sex and economics. Alec Motyer has likened the thinking behind Baal worship to

trying to teach your child to blow his nose. You take your hand-
kerchief and you make funny noises like you're blowing out of your
nose beside your child, hoping that he or she will pick up the imita-
tion. That was the idea behind Baal worship. Baal chapels would be
staffed by what could be called holy whores and you might engage in
the sex act down here and hope maybe Baal would get the cue to do
the same with his goddess counterpart in the wild blue yonder. Then
fertility would come to the earth so that crops could grow, livestock
produce and humanity produce. And of course if it worked, if there
were abundant crops, that helped economically. So Baal worship was
a lure on two fronts. It appealed to your hormones on the one hand
and it appealed to your chequebook on another. You can't really get a
religion with much more power than that. It was user-friendly. Baal
worship appealed to the felt needs of people.

This was different from the problem we met with Jeroboam.
Jeroboam put a lethal injection, with his worship, into the bloodstream
of Israel but the problem with Ahab with Baal worship was worse. It
wasn't just the syncretism of Jeroboam's worship, it was a viral vigor-
ous antipathy to faith in Yahweh.

What was typical about this unique time? I hope you caught it
from 1 Kings 16:34 about Hiel the Bethelite, who, in the days of Ahab,
rebuilt Jericho. Back in Joshua 6:26, Joshua uttered a curse on anyone
who rebuilt Jericho after Israel had destroyed it. He said, 'At the cost
of his first-born shall he lay its foundation, and at the cost of his
youngest son shall he set up its gates.' And that's what happened. Hiel
the Bethelite decided that he would apparently fly in the face of the
curse that Joshua uttered and rebuild Jericho. And he lost two of his
sons. It's as if the writer of Kings is saying, that's the way things were
in the days of Ahab. They didn't give a rip about the word of God.
'We'll fly in the face of God's word . . .' that's Ahab's regime.

What was sobering about this time?

When we think things can't get any worse, they can. You think, 'What
can get any worse than having those stupid bull calves at Dan and
Bethel and the syncretism taking place in the kingdom of Israel?' Ahab
and Jezebel come along with Baal worship and things do get worse.

What about in our own time? We think it's bad with Jesus' flock today because the flesh of Jesus' disciples is being mangled and their blood is being freely poured out across our world. If you keep up with it at all, you know that's the case, and can it get any worse? Yes, it can. Evil is capable of exponential increase. It can get worse. Jesus seems to indicate that. One of the texts that's beginning to haunt me is Luke 17:22, when Jesus says, 'The days are coming when you will desire to see one of the days of the Son of Man, and you will not see it.' In all the conflicts that you'll face, you'll wish that the Son of Man was reigning visibly in his kingdom on earth and things were put right: you'll long for that and you won't see it. It can get worse.

What was comforting?

Note where it is that you hear that evil can get worse. It is God's word that describes the excruciating times through which his people must live. That means that he knows the circumstances they are facing. If his word depicts it, if his word warns us, then he knows what his people are going to be facing. I find Revelation 2:13 a marvellous piece of reassurance: Jesus' letter to the church of Pergamum in Revelation 2:13. He says, 'I know where you dwell, where Satan's throne is.' The days are evil, and they may get more evil, but Jesus knows where we dwell.

The defence is ready (1 Kgs. 17:1)

'Now Elijah the Tishbite, of Tishbe in Gilead, said to Ahab, "As Yahweh, the God of Israel, lives, before whom I stand, there shall be neither dew nor rain these years, except by my word."' You cannot get the full effect of that unless you just keep reading from the end of chapter 16. The chapter division is very poor here in one sense.

Though it looks like Jezebel will carry the culture, out of the blue Elijah talks to Ahab and makes this announcement, in the form almost of a curse. It's so sudden and so abrupt. We're not used to this sort of thing when we read our Bibles. We expect what I call a proper King James Version introduction, something like, 'Now it came to pass that the word of the Lord came to Elijah the son of the Tishbite' and so on. But you don't have that. There's no warm-up, he's just there, and his name says it all – Elijah, Yahweh is God, it means. That's a confession of faith as well as the name of the prophet.

The message is pointed

Notice how pointed he is as well – 'there'll be no dew or rain except by my word', and notice that's introduced by an oath, 'As Yahweh, the God of Israel, lives . . .' What he announces is what we call a covenant curse. Back in Deuteronomy 11:16,17, it said that if Israel was unfaithful to the Lord and went after other gods, the Lord said that he would shut up the heavens and there would be no rain. Deuteronomy 28:23 and following indicate that in this time of Israel's unfaithfulness, the heavens would be bronze and the earth would become iron. These are not just some bad years of drought: this is the judgement of Yahweh upon Israel for their unfaithfulness.

It's more than just a covenant curse; it's a slap down on Baal, according to the view of the time. Baal was a fertility god; if there's going to be fertility, Baal has to send rain and, if he doesn't do it, the idea in popular theology was, Baal has died. Death, which was also a deity in Canaanite thinking, had been victorious over Baal. What if you cut off the rain and the dew? It's not just the rain but it's also the dew – so you won't have the autumn and the spring rains, but you also won't have the heavy dew that comes in the summers that keeps things going. It's as if Yahweh is saying, through Elijah, 'I'm going to shut Baal's faucet off.'

The message is heartening

The defence is ready. Out of nowhere comes Elijah to upfront Ahab. Think about the suddenness of that again. No sooner do evil days come in all their fury, than God provides someone to check it. It looked like all were going over to Baal, and Jezebel had the reins of Ahab's kingdom. And then there's Elijah. Sometimes it does look that way; it looks so hopeless. But the defence is ready. It's like that with God: we don't know what means he may use in any generation or situation, but he has something ready to counter the onslaught of evil in our times.

The judgement is happening (1 Kgs. 17:2–10)

As suddenly as Elijah appears, he's gone. The Lord tells him to go hide himself, doesn't he? This is an interesting section. It relates to the marvellous way in which Yahweh sustains his servant. He presses the Raven Express at Cherith into his service and they come, bringing Elijah food. Later, there is a widow in Zarephath, in the territory of Sidon. Notice the instruments God uses. He uses first of all the *unclean*. Check out Deuteronomy 14 or Leviticus 11: ravens were unclean birds. Then, not only that, he used the *unlikely*: the widow whom you would normally think was destitute. That wouldn't exactly conjure up your confidence. God uses the unclean and the unlikely to sustain his servant.

Why did Elijah hide?

Because God told him to? That's true, but why did God tell him to do it? Many think that it was in order to escape Ahab's clutches and, on the basis of chapter 18:10, there may be have been something to that, but that's not all of it. There can be more involved in something than just one reason for it. It's like that book that John F. Kennedy allegedly wrote. It came out under his name but he had something like five stenographers, a secretary and an editor. He was 23 years old and he comes out with this book, *Why England Slept* and it leaped to the best-seller list. But why? Because it sold so many copies. That's the reason. But why did it sell so many copies? Because Joe Kennedy, JFK's daddy, bought thirty to forty thousand of them and sat them in a warehouse. So sometimes there can be more reasons than one.

There's something else. Elijah disappears: who is Elijah? Elijah is the bearer of Yahweh's word. He is the one who brings it to Israel, so it's the bearer of Yahweh's word who disappears. If he does that, what does it mean? It means that Yahweh is withdrawing his word from his people. The judgement is occurring, there's no more direction or guidance at this point coming from God. His word has been despised by the regime and now it is absent. It's the sort of thing you have in Amos chapter 8 where the Lord says that he will send a famine. It won't a normal famine of bread and water but a famine of hearing the words of the Lord. When God judges a people, one of the forms of his judgement can be withdrawing his word from them. That's what you see here.

There is not just a note of judgement in Elijah's disappearance, but also in his destination. Where does he go (v. 9)? He's told to 'go to Zarephath, which belongs to Sidon', that's outside of Israel, up in Jezebel's daddy's territory. It is Gentile land, Pagansville. What's so big a deal about that? Ask the people of Nazareth, in Jesus' time. In Luke 4:25,26 in the synagogue that day, Jesus alluded to this. He said there were many widows in Israel in the days of Elijah the prophet but Elijah wasn't sent to any Israelite widow, he was sent to Zarephath. It almost got Jesus mobbed and killed. Why? Because the people got the point. What was Jesus saying? He was essentially implying that there's an act of judgement there, in which God bypassed Israel. He bypassed bringing benefit to Israel and he bestowed it upon this Gentile woman, who was not a covenant-covered Israelite. It was an act of judgement. He took his benefits away from Israel and gave them to a Baal-worshipping pagan. So what's the point?

One of the points is that God's judgement is both silent and scary. We tend to think of God's judgement as the mushroom cloud of catastrophe, of his brimstone ready to break, pulverizing men and things, but his judgement may be quiet. It may be going on right now and we may not realize it. I read in our paper, about ten years ago, that beneath the soil of one of our US national forests that's located in eastern Oregon, there's a fungus that's been slowly weaving its way through the roots of trees for centuries. It's said to have become the largest living organism ever found. It's popularly known as the honey mushroom, started from a single spore too small to be seen except with a microscope, and it's been spreading its black shoestring filaments through the forest, killing trees as it grows. It now covers some twenty-two hundred acres, but it's all very quiet.

Could God be doing this amid the professing church today? How could the Lord take away his word from us now? After all, we've got it in Scripture. And we have it so freely available. We probably have at least seventy-two different study Bibles, almost to the point where you have a study Bible for left-handed accountants. It just goes on and on and you might say, 'How can the Lord take his word away from us?'

It's not hard. I don't think the churches in the United States of America have a love affair with the word of God. There are a number of mainline denominations who make no pretence of holding to the trustworthiness of God's written word. You can visit their services and, with thankful exceptions, the word of God is absent. It's not explained or applied from the pulpit. Has it been taken away in judgement? Evangelical churches often don't seem to have any more interest in it, necessarily. They seem to be more interested in filling their teenagers' bellies with pizzas and worrying about what worship style will attract people who aren't interested anyway, than they are about sitting under the word of God. If the churches do not prize the word, then will he not withdraw the light of it and allow us to wander in the maze we so evidently prefer?

The irony is beautiful (1 Kgs.17:11–16)

Everything looked hopeless and futile, especially the demand that Elijah made of the widow when he got to Zarephath. She went to get him the water that he requested, and as she was going, he said, 'Bring me a bit of food.' Interestingly, she takes an oath by Yahweh, Elijah's God: 'As Yahweh your God lives, I have nothing baked, only a handful of flour in a jar and a little oil in a jug. And now I am gathering a couple of sticks that I may go in and prepare it for myself and my son, that we may eat it and die' (v. 12). It seems so cruel to insist that she bring him a bit of food when she was in that condition, and yet he is insistent. Elijah doesn't back down: notice the encouragement she received from him in verse 13: 'Do not fear; go and do as you have said. But first make me a little cake of it and bring it to me, and afterward make something for yourself and your son.' Then verse 14 picks up and supports the 'Do not fear' of verse 13: 'For thus says Yahweh, the God of Israel, "The jar of flour shall not be spent, and the jug of oil shall not be empty, until the day that Yahweh sends rain upon the earth." And she went and did as Elijah had said. And she and he and her household ate for many days' (vv.14,15).

It is as if Yahweh said to her, 'Give me everything you have and I will give you everything you need.' So she obeyed that word and she found Yahweh to be as reliable as his word. And this isn't a one-shot deal. Look at the last of verse 15 through verse 16, and you realize this sums up a whole period of experience. It is not that after the first evidence of faith on this woman's part, a lorry pulls up at her door with a few kilo bags of flour and five-litre containers of olive oil, and stacks them in her kitchen. It's still a day-to-day thing. She finds just a pinch of flour needed, just the amount of oil she needs for that morning. Day after day, it's another exercise of faith. God hadn't promised an overflow, he just promised that the flour and the oil would never come to an end.

When I say the irony is beautiful, who is it that Yahweh is sustaining? Who is it that receives Yahweh's promise of preserving her life? It's one of Baal's servants who now looks to the sufficiency of Yahweh for every day's need. Yahweh's newest worshipper comes out of Baal's backyard. What irony.

I remember when I was six or seven, and one of my mother's friends came to visit. Her name was Jenny and she went to prayer meetings with us, and stayed in the manse with us. She was there for several days. Jenny was an older lady, like my mother; when you're a kid, everybody's old. Apparently, she happened to notice, in the prayer meeting, one of the members of my father's congregation. His name was John Buchanan. He was probably six feet or taller and he had a deep bass voice. My dad used to brag, 'If you've got John Buchanan in your choir, you don't need any more bass.' So obviously he could make a room echo when he spoke. I don't know what it was that set my mother's friend Jenny off, but I remember her making a comment to my mother after the prayer meeting, back in the house, that she didn't like John Buchanan. Maybe she thought he was arrogant, maybe she thought he was too loud, I have no idea. Several years went by, and John Buchanan's wife died. I don't know how it happened; adults keep things hidden from kids, but next thing I know, not too long after that, my mother's friend Jenny becomes Mrs John Buchanan. That's what you call irony. I assume she got over it, whatever was the problem.

This is irony: this woman is in Baal's territory and Yahweh makes her a worshipper, a servant and a believer of his word. It's a marvellous thing, and isn't this the very same thing you see in the New Testament testimony? You have faith in the true God and Redeemer worming its way into the unwashed nooks and crannies of the world. Have you ever noticed Philippians 4:22, where the apostle says, as he's writing to the Philippians, 'All the saints greet you, especially those of Caesar's household'? There are believers in Jesus in Caesar's household. Now that doesn't mean his son and daughter and the kids, the people that are sat around his immediate table, necessarily. Caesar's household probably refers to the whole imperial civil service: they were slaves, technically. They were doctors, teachers, tutors, hairdressers: all sorts of skilled and unskilled people. But some of them had come to believe in Jesus as Lord. What irony! I wonder if Nero knew about it? Jesus had sucked them out from under Caesar's ultimate allegiance. The gospel is so subversive.

That's why people in your family get so nervous when you've just become a believer in Jesus and are willing to confess him. Why are they nervous? Well, if he's taken hold of you, they might be the next victim. Of course they're scared! Who knows what he has up his sleeve? What can't Christ do? This is why we never lose hope, because no matter how God's cause seems to be under attack in a hostile culture, Yahweh is always on the loose, calling out worshippers of his name – from the ranks of his enemies. How can you stop that?

This is the day of the Lord

What is the combined attitude we should have as we consider this testimony? As you live under anti-Christ's regime, you don't want to deny the reality and fury of evil. At the same time, you don't want to let your gaze slip from the Redeemer who rules it all. I think maybe it was summed up in a clip from the diary of a Dutch woman, during September 1944. I believe it was during what they call the Market Garden Offensive in Holland. There were British medics who were trying to work with probably both British and maybe American and German prisoners, in a hotel in a town in Holland. One of the Dutch volunteers was a woman. She was helping nurse some of these wounded, and she has an entry in her diary for Sunday 24 September. This is what it says: 'This is the day of the Lord. War rages outside. The building is shaking.' She goes on to explain that's why the doctors can't operate or fix casts: 'We cannot wash the wounded because nobody can venture out to find water under these conditions.' Did you see how she put it, on that Lord's Day morning? 'This is the day of the Lord. War rages outside. The building is shaking.'

You need to realize always that in a hostile culture, war rages outside, the building is shaking, but never forget the first statement: 'This is the day of the Lord.'

4. Enduring the perplexity of God: 1 Kings 17:17–24

Introduction

Sergeant Henderson Verdon was a soldier in the Confederate army in our war between the states, serving in the Second Arkansas. He was off serving for a year in the army, marching around, and never saw or heard from his wife and children for that year. Then gradually, he seemed to be coming back to what was familiar territory, marching over ground that he knew about. They were back in Arkansas, and he was involved in the battle of Pea Ridge in 1862. Sergeant Verdon was wounded in that battle. They were fighting on his own farm and he was wounded there. He was carried into his own house and his own wife tended him until he could return to his regiment.

Sometimes something like war becomes very personal, and that's the way it is with our theme of living by faith in a fallen world. We need to know where that fallenness begins, and so in our first episode in 1 Kings 11, we talked about Solomon and the fact that the fallenness in our fallen world begins in our own heart. In that fallen world, we meet self-styled religion, like the perversions of Jeroboam and, even worse, we can come under a regime that makes it look like anti-Christ has already come. But when we come to 1 Kings 17:17–24, it's as if living by faith in a fallen world gets quite individual; when it seems like that world falls in on me.

It didn't seem like that at Zarephath at the beginning. This widow had a daily experience of God's faithfulness. God had marvellously provided for her, her son and Elijah, and she couldn't help but be grateful for that. But in one of Charles Schultz's Peanuts cartoons, there's one of those episodes in which Lucy is reading a story to Linus, and she reads, 'And so the king was granted his wish. Everything he touched would turn to gold. Now the next day . . .' At that point, Linus jumps up and exclaims, 'Stop! You don't have to go any further. I know what's just going to happen.' And he walks away moaning, 'These things always have a way of backfiring.' That's what you see in our text. You read that phrase in verse 17, 'Now it came about after these things' (NASB) and you say, 'I know what's going to happen. Things change.' Sometimes our troubles are at the macro level, the kingdom of God level, and we're facing an Ahab and a Jezebel. But sometimes our troubles are at the micro level and we wonder how Yahweh is ruling (or perhaps not ruling) in our circumstances. Here we face the question that the text forces upon us: 'Can I live by faith in a fallen world when that world falls in on me?'

The problem of God's ways (1 Kgs. 17:17,18)

> After this the son of the woman, the mistress of the house, became ill. And his illness was so severe that there was no breath left in him. And she said to Elijah, 'What have you against me, O man of God? You have come to me to bring my sin to remembrance and to cause the death of my son!'

We've called this the problem of God's ways but in one sense, this is not a problem. In Job 1:21, Job, after his losses, says, 'Yahweh gave, and Yahweh has taken away; blessed be the name of Yahweh.' In one sense, he's right. Job seemed to have the understanding that every-thing he had, as someone has said, was a gift of grace. Everything he had, had been given to him and, if all of life is grace, if everything I have is God's gift, then if he takes it, it's his perfect right to do so. What claim do I have on anything that's been given by his grace?

How can I hold on to it? What God gives, he has a right to take, if he so pleases.

Yet here, contextually, it *is* a problem. Here is this woman, humming as she goes about her work in the kitchen, singing about God being so good to her. Then this happens. What is God up to, when he apparently takes the life of her son? Does God do good to us, only to make our distress more galling? Does he lift us up and show us his mercy and his kindness and his provision, so that when he drops us, we'll hit with a harder thud? Is that what is happening here? Sometimes we wonder about that.

Back in about 1949, in our US House of Representatives, there was a freshman congressman by the name of Gross. He was from Iowa and he was worrying a bit because he hadn't yet made his initial speech in the House of Representatives. He happened to mention this to a veteran congressman from Michigan, a guy by the name of Hoffman. Hoffman said to Gross, 'There's nothing to making that maiden speech in the House. I'm making a long speech tomorrow and, somewhere in it, you stop me and ask a question. I'll answer it and that will take care of your first speech. You'll have your feet wet in the water.' Gross was elated by Hoffman's kindness to him, and he rehearsed with him the question he was supposed to ask and the exact point in Hoffman's speech where he was to interrupt.

So the next day Hoffman was making his speech in the House, and Gross rose and asked if the congressman from Michigan would yield for a question. And Hoffman courteously yielded. Gross then posed his question and sat down to wait for the answer. He never forgot Hoffman's reply. It was, 'I cannot understand what possessed the gentleman from Iowa to ask such a stupid question!' He had simply set him up. Sometimes, though we might not be that crass, we tend to think that perhaps the Lord does that. Perhaps he shows goodness and mercy so that the contrast will be all the worse. Could he use mercy in almost a cruel sense, in the light of the following disaster that comes to this woman – the everlasting jar of flour and then the devastating death of her son? Does Yahweh give the means to sustain life (vv. 8–16) only to take away one of the lives he sustains? What's going on here?

God's ways seem to be inconsistent: note who it is on whom the Lord inflicts this. It's on a new convert! She has just barely escaped from the clutches of Baal, she's just come to know the goodness of Yahweh and his mighty provision in the face of famine, she's just come out of paganism. It wasn't as if the Lord chose a mature believer, who had a history of coping with adversity. What on earth is God doing here?

Then there comes the inescapable question of guilt and punishment, in verse 18, when she says: 'What have you against me, O man of God? You have come to me to bring my sin to remembrance and to cause the death of my son!' We may say we would never get to that point, because we remember John 9:3, when Jesus said of that man born blind, 'Neither this man nor his parents sinned . . . but this happened so that the work of God might be displayed in his life.' But you'd be surprised what you think when you're down in the middle of the mire in the pit. You conjure up all sorts of things you haven't thought of for years that the Lord might be holding against you. John 9:3 will never cross your radar screen. Somehow you'll completely lose Psalm 103: 'He does not deal with us according to our sins, nor repay us according to our iniquities' (v. 10). Or, if you do, you'll be sure that it doesn't carry your address. It's for somebody else.

The doctrine of the perplexity of God

What you have here is the apparent inconsistency of God and it teaches a doctrine which I wish more of the theological textbooks would include: the doctrine of the perplexity of God. I run into it all the time in the Scripture and I think it needs to be up there in our systematic theologies, with some of the doctrine of the Trinity and with the mercy of God and his various attributes. The doctrine of the perplexity of God: don't you see it here? But notice where is it that you meet this. It's in 1 Kings 17. The Bible itself presses this matter of God's perplexity and mystery on you. It tells you that you'll be tied in knots sometimes, wondering what sin God might be punishing. It tells you that sometimes you'll wonder, 'Why do I go through such favour and delight with the Lord and then comes bleak Tuesday?' Why is there sometimes an 'after these things' episode? It's as if the Scripture is trying to say, 'Can you deal with this thing vicariously in the Scripture before you have to face it experientially?' The Bible makes us face the problem of God's ways. I think this text is not so disturbing as it is comforting. It is teaching you that God is not always crystal clear in your circumstances. You see it in the Scripture.

The humility of God's servant (1 Kgs. 17:19–22a)

> And he said to her, 'Give me your son.' And he took him from her arms and carried him up into the upper chamber where he lodged, and laid him on his own bed. And he cried to Yahweh, 'O Yahweh my God, have you brought calamity even upon the widow with whom I sojourn, by killing her son?' Then he stretched himself upon the child three times and cried to Yahweh, 'O Yahweh my God, let this child's life come into him again.' And Yahweh listened to the voice of Elijah.

Elijah could do with a little training: notice in verse 19 he doesn't exactly have the pastoral touch: 'Give me your son.' He could have done better. But he takes him up, and notice how twice it says that he called to Yahweh (vv. 20,21). Look at Elijah's words in verse 20, when he says, '. . . have you brought calamity even upon the widow with whom I sojourn, by killing her son?' Compare those words in verse 20 with the widow's words in verse 18: 'What have you against me, O man of God? You have come to me to bring my sin to remembrance and to cause the death of my son!' Elijah doesn't exactly repeat her words but he does take up her thought and her concern. I find that interesting. If you look at verse 20 in the light of verse 18, notice how Elijah expresses the very anguish of the widow in his prayer. I wonder if we ever pray like that, from the other person's point of view? Do we pray with that sort of imagination, pleading their anguish before God? Elijah here takes up the anguish of the woman almost as his own and expresses it to Yahweh on her behalf.

Notice the view we have of Elijah here. Is Elijah a courageous prophet? Yes: you see that especially in chapter 18, but notice that he doesn't have some slick trick up his sleeve. He doesn't have a sleazy, easy money-making offer that he can give this woman if she just has her credit card ready and calls this number immediately. He doesn't have any of that; there's no magic with him. You may say, 'What is this about him stretching himself upon the child?' I think that's an acted prayer. It comes in between the two times in which it says he called out to Yahweh – the two expressions of Elijah's prayer. I take his stretching himself upon the lad as a kind of prophetic action that reinforces the prayer. Note how everything rests on verse 22: 'And Yahweh listened to the voice of Elijah.' That's what really matters in prayer.

Elijah is simply a prophet-servant. He's not a magician; he's not an easy-answer man; he simply begs Yahweh for this mighty work. Elijah is reduced to prayer, to begging from God. Sometimes it's a great encouragement to us to see that people that we tend to think are somehow great, share our own weaknesses and limitations. I know that kind of thinking can go to seed at times, but nevertheless it's sometimes a big encouragement to us.

Charles XII, the King of Sweden, was only 18 years old and he thought that he and his fellow Swedish army folks needed to attack the Russians on the Baltic Sea. He was leading a little over ten thousand Swedish troops, in November, which wasn't a very good time. The roads were boggy and the autumn rains were coming. The men had to march in deep, thick, syrupy mud, and sometimes sleep in it. As they went on their march, they came to burned out Russian farmsteads because the Russians had burned everything to keep the Swedish army from getting supplies. So there was no fodder, no food, except what they had in their knapsacks, and there was a steady cold November rain that fell during the day. Then, as the temperatures dropped later into the evening, there would be flurries of sleet and snow, and the ground would begin to freeze at night.

Robert Massie, in his book on Peter the Great, has an interesting statement as he gives this whole setting: 'The king slept with his men under the open sky receiving the rain and snow on his face.'[3] Charles XII slept, like the privates did, in the muck. He didn't have a nice palatial tent or a roaring fire that would keep him warm. He slept there under the sleet and the snow, just like his men did. You have to respect that. That's what you see in Elijah: one who has to beg Yahweh in prayer to answer him.

You may want a prophetic ministry: here you see one. People are often described as having a prophetic ministry – what that often means is that they are really good at chewing out the Lord's people. Sometimes that's the tone that that can take. But if you want a prophetic ministry, you've got one here. Elijah simply pleads with Yahweh in prayer; that's the God-appointed means of grace for our difficulties. Remember James 5:13? 'Is anyone among you suffering? Let him pray. Is anyone cheerful? Let him sing praise.' No matter what circumstances you're in, you're called to respond to God. If you're suffering, you pray; if you're happy and cheerful, you sing praise to God who gives you the cheerfulness and the happiness. As Calvin says of that text, 'There is no time in which God does not invite us to himself.' Whatever our circumstances are, God is trying to suck our attention and our worship toward him. Are we suffering? We pray. Are we cheerful? We praise.

James picks up on Elijah in James 5:17, in another connection. He says that Elijah prayed that it might not rain, and it did not rain. Then he prayed again, and the rain came. The Greek text of James 5:17 is often translated 'He prayed earnestly'. Literally, it's 'with prayer he prayed'. That an interesting idea. You might ask yourself, 'Do I pray in my prayers?' Alec Motyer makes the point in his commentary: it's not so much that James is saying he prayed earnestly, but he just *prayed*. Now you may not be a prophet, and you may not be a son of a prophet, but you can have the ministry of a prophet, begging God on behalf of others in intercessory prayer. There's your prophetic ministry.

The revelation for God's people (1 Kgs. 17:22b–24)

And the life of the child came into him again, and he revived. And Elijah took the child and brought him down from the upper chamber into the house and delivered him to his mother. And Elijah said, 'See, your son lives.' And the woman said to Elijah, 'Now I know that you are a man of God, and that the word of Yahweh in your mouth is truth.'

The word truth – '. . . the word of Yahweh in your mouth is truth' –
I think the writer here is using it in what you might call an adjectival
way: 'The word of Yahweh in your mouth is reliable.'

A general revelation

I think there are two elements in this revelation for God's people. First
of all, there's what we might call a general revelation regarding our trials. Notice the insight that the widow gained. She now had confidence once more in the reliability of Yahweh. 'The word of truth, the
word of Yahweh in your mouth, is reliable.' In the face of his per-
plexing and seemingly absurd and contradictory way of sustaining her,
and then taking away the life of one he had sustained, Yahweh showed
himself reliable in the end after all. That's the assurance: in the face of
God's seemingly inconsistent ways, at the end of our trials, he will
show himself faithful to his people. That's what James 5:11 indicates:
'Behold, we consider those blessed who remained steadfast. You have
heard of the steadfastness of Job, and you have seen the purpose of the
Lord, how the Lord is compassionate and merciful.'

It says, 'You have heard of the steadfastness of Job, and you have
seen the purpose of the Lord' – I think also of that text in
Deuteronomy 8:16 where Moses is speaking to Israel about how God
cared for them from the exodus and so on. He refers to God as the
one 'who fed you in the wilderness with manna that your fathers did
not know, that he might humble you and test you, to do you good in
the end.' When you see the whole package, the end shows him to be
reliable. You may have trouble figuring it all out in the midst of all the
mess at the time, but you see what the Lord finally brings about. So
as she sees that here, she sees that she will be able to trust Yahweh
again.

It was Donald Grey Barnhouse who used to tell the story of the
time when he came over to England, in his late twenties. He visited
Winchester Cathedral and there was a verger who liked to explain the
story of how word came from the Battle of Waterloo, back to
England. There were no telegraph facilities in those days and so they
would signal by flag. So a ship would do the flag signals to someone
on the top of Winchester Cathedral and then he would signal to

someone on a hill beyond him, and so it would go. (Now, you English people may know that this is not right, but just pretend it is!) You would keep signalling until the message got to London, and eventually to all England.

Finally a sailing ship came into sight and it began signalling to the guy on Winchester Cathedral. The first word was 'Wellington' and the second word was 'defeated'. And then a fog came in and you couldn't see the ship. So 'Wellington defeated' went across England and, according to Barnhouse, all England was in gloom. Then after two or three hours the fog lifted and the ship was still there. It was signalling the words: 'Wellington defeated the enemy' and all England rejoiced.

That's sometimes the way it is. You see that the Lord really has been faithful at the end of the trial, but often we live in the fog in the middle of it. We can't yet see what he designs to bring about. That's the general revelation here from the widow's situation, I think, to ours.

Specific revelation

I think there's also a specific revelation here regarding the 'great' trial: that is, death. This episode shows that Yahweh is not only victor over dearth but over death. He not only preserves this widow and her son in the face of the famine (vv. 8–16), but he also shows that he has the power over death and can reverse death (vv. 17–24). It is not the time yet for the final victory over death but here the Lord, through his answer to Elijah's prayer, gives a sneak preview of what is to come. God gives us more such tokens in the New Testament. Episodes in the ministry of Jesus are meant to say essentially the same thing. In Mark 5:35, as they came from Jairus' house: ' "Your daughter is dead," they said. "Why bother the teacher any more?" ' But Jesus went to the house and brought Jairus' daughter back to life and told them to feed her lunch. There in Mark chapters 4 and 5, you have a whole series of the mighty acts of Jesus. It begins in Mark 4:35–41 where you see Jesus supreme over creation, as the storm rages on the Sea of Galilee, and the disciples are afraid they're perishing. There you see Jesus supreme over danger. Then you get into Mark 5:1–20, the very next passage, and you see Jesus restoring this man called Legion: Jesus supreme over demons. Then you see that woman with an issue of blood, sneaking around behind in the crowd: Jesus supreme over disease. Then you hear the terrible report from Jairus' house about his daughter being dead and you see Jesus supreme over death. Here's the one who's supreme over all realms – over danger, demons, disease and death. Mark means by that coalition of stories to stand and say, 'Hallelujah, what a Saviour he is.'

The impact of that story with Jairus' daughter in Mark 5 is the same as the thrust of 1 Kings 17:17–24. It's really saying, 'Here's a sample. Here's the sort of thing that Christ does. You enter the realm of death, you are not beyond the reach of Jesus' power or the sound of his voice.' Just as Yahweh is supreme over death in 1 Kings 17, so is Jesus.

Why don't we have more episodes like that? It's not time for it yet. That's the same reason you don't have many instances of the restoration to life from the dead in the biblical period either. You have some, but Jesus didn't empty the cemeteries or anything like that. It was relatively rare. They were meant to be signs, and we still have that comfort.

The time when the resurrection is going to occur is at the second coming of Jesus, 1 Thessalonians 4: 'And the dead in Christ will rise first. Then we who are alive' (vv. 16,17). But even there you see the hope, in that little hyphenated phrase that the apostle Paul uses in verse 16 when he says, 'the dead in Christ will rise first.' They're not dead, they're dead-in-Christ. In their death, they are linked in union with the living Saviour and Redeemer. You can't be finally dead if you're dead and united with Christ in your death. There has to be a resurrection. That's why you have what Jesus offers you in John 6:39: 'And this is the will of him who sent me, that I should lose nothing of all that he has given me, but raise it up on the last day.'

How could he lose anything? Could some of his people slip through his hands, drop through the black hole of the universe in death, and never be recovered? Can they be lost through death? Jesus says, 'No. My father's will is that of all that he's given me, I should lose nothing but raise it up at the last day.' That is our hope.

I still love the story that James Stewart, the Scottish preacher, told. I think it's in one of his books, about Faust, in the old story, who gambled with his soul. James Stewart said that an artist has painted a picture of that game of chess, Faust on one side and Satan on the other. The game in the picture is almost over, Faust has only a few pieces left, a king, a knight, one or two pawns, and on his face is this look of blank despair. At the other side of the chessboard, the devil leers in anticipation of his triumph. And he said that many a chess player had looked at the picture and agreed that the position is hopeless; it's checkmate. But one day, he said, there was a great master of the game who stood gazing at the picture in the gallery. He was fascinated by that look of terrible despair on the face of Faust and then his gaze went down to the pieces on the board. He stared at them, absorbed. Other visitors to the gallery came and went, and still he was preoccupied and fixated by the pieces on the board, lost in contemplation. Then suddenly there was a ringing shout from the chess master: 'It's all right! The king and the knight have another move.'

That's the way it is with death. Jesus always has the last move. What he is telling you through the widow of Zarephath and through the episode of Jairus' daughter is that, even though you enter into the realm of death, you do not go beyond the sound of his voice or the reach of a nail-scarred hand. He has the keys of death and of Hades. And you have a foregleam of that, right here within the city limits of Zarephath.

So, can I live by faith in a fallen world when that world seems to fall in on me? When I can't seem to make heads or tail of what God is doing? I think we have to ask a question: To whom can we go? Only, as the text says, to the God who perplexes us, who hears us, and who will raise us.

5. Servants of God under the oppression of man: 1 Kings 21

A number of years ago there was a story in the *Daily Bread* devotional magazine of a professor who taught philosophy, who asked his students if they thought there was such a thing as absolute values, like justice for instance. Most of them said no, everything is relative. There's no law or principle that's valid at all times for everyone. He said that they would discuss this before the class was over in the semester, and so one day he set aside a class period. Apparently all of the students felt that there were no absolutes and so he said, 'Nevertheless, no matter what you say, I want you to know that absolute values can be demonstrated and if you don't agree with what I say, I'll flunk you.' One student was so angered by that that he got up, walked out of the class and, as he did, he said, 'That's not fair.' You may need to think about that for a little bit.

There are always those who think that there is no such thing as right and wrong. If you ever meet one, all you have to do is stomp really hard on their toe, and they will at least believe in wrong. One of the ravages of our fallen world is the matter of injustice, and you have a sample of it in 1 Kings 21. I'm not sure that the text tells us how to live by faith under injustice, but it points us to trust the God of justice. So this will not be three strategies for coping with unfairness in your life, but rather the testimony of the text is essentially that of Luke 18:7,8 and the words of Jesus, 'And will not God give justice to his elect, who cry to him day and night? Will he delay long over them? I tell you, he will give justice to them speedily.'

Realization (1 Kgs. 21:1–7)

The first point I want to make is to be summed up in the term realization, and the principle is, 'God's people must expect to suffer injustice in this world.' We're in about 860BC in the kingdom of Israel, the northern kingdom, Ahab is king and he's married to Jezebel, his hard-hearted, Baal-worshipping, mascara-laden wife whom we've already met. Verses 1–4

> Now Naboth the Jezreelite had a vineyard in Jezreel, beside the palace of Ahab king of Samaria. And after this Ahab said to Naboth, 'Give me your vineyard, that I may have it for a vegetable garden, because it is near my house, and I will give you a better vineyard for it; or, if it seems good to you, I will give you its value in money.' But Naboth said to Ahab, 'Yahweh forbid that I should give you the inheritance of my fathers.' And Ahab went into his house vexed and sullen because of what Naboth the Jezreelite had said to him, for he had said, 'I will not give you the inheritance of my fathers.' And he lay down on his bed and turned away his face and would eat no food.

Ahab makes what he probably thinks is a reasonable offer to Naboth in Jezreel. He wanted his vineyard: it was close to his palace and he wanted it for a vegetable garden. But Naboth says, 'Yahweh forbid that I should give you the inheritance of my fathers.' He didn't mean 'give': this was in the sense of 'selling to'. He is arguing, I think, on the basis of Leviticus 25:23–28, and texts like Numbers 36:7–9. There was an arrangement whereby if a man became too poor and had to sell his inherited land, he could do that with the option that it could be redeemed at a later time. Naboth is thinking if there's no necessity to do that, he should not give the inheritance of his fathers to Ahab. He was perfectly within his rights there. Notice that he seems to identify himself as a subject of Yahweh. He seems to be a member of what we sometimes call the believing remnant in Israel, holding to God's word.

Ahab goes home in a pout. It was only a vineyard and Ahab didn't need it, but he is 'vexed and sullen'. He was resentful and raging. That's the problem, and it leads into a conversation. Jezebel comes to see him and wonders why he's looking at the wall. He tells her what Naboth told him but he just says that Naboth said, 'I will not give you my vineyard.' Maybe he didn't want to explain about the inheritance of the fathers, maybe he thought Jezebel, being a pagan, wouldn't understand, or maybe he wanted to make Naboth look a little worse.

Notice how Jezebel has a different world-view from an Israelite world-view. In verse 7, as the New Jerusalem Bible translates it, 'Some king of Israel you make! Get up, eat and take heart; I myself shall get you the vineyard of Naboth'. Translation: 'No local yokel grape-picker is going to stand in the way of this regime. Where I come from,' Jezebel says, 'kings get what they want. If they don't want to give it to you, you take it. Wise up!' So that leads to the action of verses 8 through 14. She goes into Ahab's office and gets his letterheads and his seal and she writes letters to the leaders and magistrates in Naboth's town. I take that to be somewhere in the area of Jezreel, if not Jezreel itself.

They do what Jezebel says, but notice the legality of it all. It's a religious occasion. Jezebel says, proclaim a fast, put Naboth in a prominent place among the people and then bring two scumbags in who will serve as witnesses and accuse him of cursing God and the king. Then you take him out and stone him to death. Notice she was very careful to make sure there were two witnesses, because as Deuteronomy says, you can't condemn someone on the testimony of one witness. They knew better than to try to oppose Jezebel's orders and so they did what she said. They sent word to her that Naboth was dead. In fact, 2 Kings 9:26 tells us that at this time they also wiped out Naboth's sons. You can't just get rid of Naboth: he's got sons who could inherit the vineyard, so you have to liquidate the whole lot.

What are the implications of this, about suffering injustice in this world? We must understand that this is a typical narrative. It is not merely about Naboth and Jezebel and Ahab but this is a true picture of the lot of the people of God in this world. Very often this will be the case. 1 Peter 4:12,13 teaches: 'Beloved, do not be surprised at the fiery trial when it comes upon you to test you, as though something strange were happening to you. But rejoice insofar as you share Christ's sufferings, that you may also rejoice and be glad when his glory is revealed.'

This is what we can frequently expect. We shouldn't be surprised. There's a lot of counter-Christian propaganda out there. The prosperity gospel, if you call that a gospel, says things like this, 'I believe that it is the plan of God our Father that no believer should ever be sick.' Another says not even a headache, not even a toothache should come your way. I think Naboth would be surprised at that kind of thing.

Someone who I think would understand 1 Kings 21 easily was Richard Wurmbrand. After he had been thrown in the slammer of the Communist prisons in Eastern Europe for fourteen years, when he was released finally, he was in Romania in the early 1960s. He was a Lutheran pastor and he was constantly followed and watched. He tells about one Sunday, taking a group of children to the Bucharest zoo. He said secret police agents followed but stayed at the gate when he took the children into the zoo. He said he led the children, who were going to be confirmed soon, to the lions' cage, and gathered them around him so he could speak to them quietly. This is what he said: 'Your forefathers in the faith were thrown to wild animals like these. They died gladly because they believed in Jesus. The time may come when you, too, will be imprisoned and suffer for being a Christian. Now you must decide whether you're ready to face that day.' He said that was the only question he asked in his last confirmation class, in Romania.

Not only is this a typical narrative of what can be our common and frequent lot but it also implies, beware of the government. Such injustice as you see here comes from Ahab and Jezebel, from the top: from the government or its agencies. Go with Elijah into 2 Kings 1 and it comes from King Ahaziah, Ahab's son, who tried to liquidate Elijah. Go to Jeremiah 36 and the opposition trying to crush the word of God comes from King Jehoiakim of Judah. Go to Daniel 3 and the opposition comes from the mega-power Babylon. Go to Revelation

2 and 3 and it comes from Rome and the emperor worship threat.
Watch for that as you go through the Scriptures.

Former president Ronald Reagan in the United States referred to
what he called the nine most terrifying words in the English language.
'I'm from the government and I'm here to help.' Now you're going to
say, 'Davis, you're just a cynical American' and that's true. But also
you're saying, 'You're being subversive. Aren't you to remember
Romans 13 and 1 Peter 2? Aren't you to respect and honour government and government officials?' Yes. 'Aren't you to pray for those in
high positions (1 Tim. 2)?' Yes. But does the Bible ever tell you to trust
the government? We offer respect and honour, when honour is due.
Pray for government officials but don't trust the government: that's an
implication.

Another implication is that we have a 'Naboth' who understands
and knows our position. It's interesting to put verse 13 of our text
beside another text that we know, when two 'worthless men' come in,
false witnesses, to bring the charge against Naboth. In Matthew
26:59–61, Jesus of Nazareth was standing before the Jewish authorities and they were trying to find witnesses. They couldn't find any and
then at last there were two witnesses who brought false charges. What
is that but Jesus being in a Naboth situation? Don't you read about
that in Isaiah 53? 'He was oppressed, and he was afflicted, yet he
opened not his mouth . . . By oppression and judgement he was taken
away; and as for his generation, who considered that he was cut off out
of the land of the living, stricken for the transgression of my people?'
(Isa. 53:7,8)

What's that say to us? If you are in Naboth's position, you are not
isolated: Christ is united to you. He has stood in Naboth's place. He
knows what it is to be falsely accused. God's people must expect to
suffer injustice in this world: that's the realization.

Admonition (1 Kgs. 21:8–14)

The principle there is God's servants must be prepared to pay the
price of standing for justice. All of this could have been stopped. These

local magistrates could have refused to play along, but they knuckled under and did as Jezebel had sent word to them. Why didn't they take a stand against Jezebel? Why didn't they expose her scheme? What would've happened if they refused, though? The Mafia in Samaria would have liquidated them, and they knew that. There would have been a price to pay. Injustice flourishes not only by wickedness but by weakness: not merely from the lack of goodness but from a lack of guts. The problem is, here is the fear of man or, in this case, of woman. Jesus told us about this. See Matthew 10:28.

At the root of the matter is idolatry. You can understand what they were facing. They were thinking, 'I've got to live.' Sometimes Satan's lie can come to say to us, 'You have to survive, so command these stones to become loaves of bread.' We have to be careful, and graciously God doesn't always require this of us, but I need to be careful that my own preservation does not become my god. God's servants must be prepared to pay the price of standing for justice.

Consolation (1 Kgs. 21:17–24)

The principle there is God will intervene to bring justice to his wronged people. After verse 16, everything has turned out the way Jezebel had designed it. But then you read an interesting thing: 'Then the word of Yahweh came to Elijah the Tishbite' (v. 17). Notice the assumption that's operating here, when a word of Yahweh intervenes through Elijah. It is that no one is exempt from the scrutiny and the judgement of God's word, not even royalty. They're subject to the word of God: they're not exempt. They too stand under the floodlight of God's omniscience, and God has seen.

There are always some who think they don't have to be subject to God's law. The Kennedys were a prominent family in New England and Rose Kennedy, JFK's mother, was chauffeured by a fellow by the name of Frank Saunders. When she was reading the newspapers in the back seat of the car, Rose Kennedy had a habit of throwing the finished papers out of the window. Saunders warned Rose Kennedy that they could get picked up for littering, and they could be fined. And

Rose said, 'Oh Frank, they know who we are.' What an amazing assumption, isn't it? We're the family of the president, we're not subject to common regulations. That's what Ahab and Jezebel may have thought, but they are not exempt from the scrutiny and the judgement of God's word.

Now, look at the consolation here, especially in verses 18 and 19.

> Arise, go down to meet Ahab king of Israel, who is in Samaria; behold, he is in the vineyard of Naboth, where he has gone to take possession. And you shall say to him, 'Thus says Yahweh, "Have you killed and also taken possession?' And you shall say to him, 'Thus says Yahweh: "In the place where dogs licked up the blood of Naboth shall dogs lick your own blood." '

Yahweh did not let it pass. He saw and he intervened, he interrupted in the process. This is the same God as you see in Exodus 3:7 where Yahweh said to Moses, 'I have surely seen the affliction of my people who are in Egypt and have heard their cry because of their taskmasters. I know their sufferings'. There was no airtight cover-up here.

One writer says that after it stated that Naboth died, Naboth's name occurs six times in the next three verses. He may be dead but he is not forgotten by his God. Naboth bites the dust as a helpless victim, but Yahweh is the God who sees their lifeless forms lying amongst the stones. He is the same God who sees in Myanmar when the military use Christians, especially women and girls, as human minesweepers to go in front of the army. It doesn't really matter if they get maimed or blown to bits because they are Christians. They are getting away with it, apparently, but there is the God of Elijah who's watching. Then there is that North Korean family who disappeared. Their 10-year-old daughter was in school and her teacher asked her how it was that she was able to get such a good grade on her paper. She said, 'By God's grace' and no one has apparently seen or heard of her or her parents since that day. But the God of Elijah has seen.

You may find small consolation here, because you say, 'God interrupted and intervened and called Ahab and Jezebel to account, but he didn't save Naboth's skin.' It didn't look like God protected Naboth.

There is a double pattern in the Scripture. In Acts chapter 12, you see James, of James and John Fishing Company, executed by Herod Agrippa. And you have Peter thrown in the slammer and he's going to be brought out and executed, but is marvellously delivered from prison. What's the problem? Did James not have enough faith? Was he defective in his faith and that's why Herod Agrippa got him? No, don't go down there: you can't find that in the text. You have the marvellous providence of God working on behalf of Peter, and you have the mysterious providence of God working in James' situation. One apostle is executed and the other is marvellously set free.

Go to Matthew 2: Jesus was a toddler and Joseph was told to take the family to Egypt because Herod was seeking to kill the child. Herod's police came down to the area round Bethlehem and they butchered all the toddlers 2 years old and under. Think of the homes in which misery and grief and tears flowed freely. Jesus was rescued, Jesus found refuge in Egypt. The Saviour was saved, but what about all those families in Bethlehem that didn't have any marvellous deliverance? God didn't send anyone to warn them in a dream to get out of there. You have mysterious providence in their situation, and marvellous providence in Jesus' situation, but there's no guarantee of some sort of immunity. We crave immunity, but God doesn't always stop injustice in its tracks. He may give us marvellous deliverance, and he may not. The Lord gives us security but we want more, we want immunity.

The Naboth episode shows us that we have no guarantee of immunity from injustice but only that at some point we will receive justice. Isn't it 2 Thessalonians 1:6 and following that tells us when we will get justice, '. . . since indeed God considers it just to repay with affliction those who afflict you, and to grant relief to you who are afflicted as well as to us, when the Lord Jesus is revealed from heaven with his mighty angels in flaming fire, inflicting vengeance on those who do not know God and on those who do not obey the gospel of our Lord Jesus.' A day is coming when the Judge will come and he will put things right for his suffering people.

In spite of the mysteries, in spite of the fact that Naboth hasn't got justice, still I would call this consolation. God will intervene to bring justice to his wronged people. I think that was highlighted in something that Chris Wright said, some probably fifteen years ago, in an article. He'd been speaking at a conference in India and a fellow came up to him afterwards who was at that time a doctor of science and a university lecturer in chemistry. He came up to tell Dr Wright how thrilled he was to hear that he was going to be speaking on the Old Testament at this conference because, he said, he had become a Christian by reading the Old Testament. How does that happen? Let Chris Wright tell.

> This man grew up in one of the backward and oppressed groups of India. He was a part of a community that was always exploited and crushed and trampled upon, treated with contempt and sometimes violence, and this worked in him as a youth as a burning desire for vengeance and revenge . . . He gave himself to his education so that he could better himself. He committed himself to Marxism along the way. His desire was to get to such a place that he could turn the tables on those who had treated him with such contempt and with such harm. When he went to his university though he met some Christian students and they gave him a Bible and he decided out of casual interest that he was going to read the Bible. The first thing that he happened to read in the Bible was the story of Naboth, Ahab and Jezebel in 1 Kings 21. He said he was astonished to find it was all about greed for land, abuse of power, corruption of the courts, violence against the poor – things that he was all too familiar with. Even more amazing was the fact that God took Naboth's side and not only accused Ahab and Jezebel of their wrongdoing but took vengeance on them. And his response was, 'I never knew such a God existed.'

Here was a God he could respect, a God he felt attracted to, one who took the side of the oppressed and took direct action against their enemies. 'I never knew such a God existed.' I hope you can feel something of the attractiveness of a God of justice that cares.

Invitation (1 Kgs. 21:25–29)

Here the principle is, 'God delights to exercise mercy while imposing his justice'. Here was a man who was sold out to evil. I think the ESV is probably right, it puts verses 25 and 26 in brackets, because verse 27 picks up the flow of the narrative from verse 24. After the terrible judgement that Elijah announces on Ahab and Jezebel, and on Ahab's dynasty, it says in verses 27–29

> And when Ahab heard those words, he tore his clothes and put sack-cloth on his flesh and fasted and lay in sackcloth and went about dejectedly. And the word of Yahweh came to Elijah the Tishbite, say-ing, 'Have you seen how Ahab has humbled himself before me? Because he has humbled himself before me, I will not bring the disas-ter in his days; but in his son's days I will bring the disaster upon his house.'

In verses 25 and 26, here is a man sold out to evil and yet he was apparently moved to some degree of repentance in verse 27. You may be disappointed with God here. You may be saying, why is God so gullible? You're a sophisticated, cynical, evangelical Christian who doesn't trust these phoney repentance guys. Any Christian with a decent degree of legalism in his make-up says, 'But did Ahab *really* repent?' That's our question, isn't it, here? It's as if the Lord says to Elijah (v. 29), 'Did you see that? Look at Ahab, he's got sackcloth on! He's going around moping. He's really touched with sorrow. So I'm not going to bring the disaster in his days, I'll bring it in his son's days.'

It doesn't mean that he cancels the judgement, it means he delays it; there's a difference between cancellation and postponement. God postpones the judgement to a later point but it's still on the books. But he seems so willing to show mercy to Ahab.

I wonder if verse 29 was communicated to Ahab? Obviously it was communicated to Elijah and I think probably verse 29 was commu-nicated to Ahab. I would think Elijah would pass on that the judge-ment would come not in his days, but in his son's days. That's the Lord's way of taking account of the degree of repentance at least that

Ahab showed. Was there anything lasting about that repentance? I think it was probably in earnest for the time. I think it made a real impression on Ahab. I don't think it was likely that it was long-lasting, but it did wake him up, it did make him think, it did give an emotional sorrow that went on for some time, and the Lord was willing to take account of that. It's as if James 4:8 is operating, 'Draw near to God, he'll draw near to you.' Ahab makes some degree of response. Maybe it's not total, maybe it's not even going to be genuine or long-lasting, but see how willing God seems to be to extend mercy to the least trifle of repentance. We draw near to God in our own temporary and muddled way, but God's willing to draw near to us in the face of that.

Does not this mercy beckon Ahab to seek more mercy? Shouldn't it have made him think that if the Lord postpones the judgement based on his response at this point, maybe he could receive more mercy if he cast himself on the mercy of this God of justice? Who knows what Yahweh might be willing to do? He always seems to have such an enthusiasm over showing mercy on the slightest pretext. He seems to be trigger-happy to show mercy. That's what he does here, to the degree that Ahab should have sensed an invitation to throw himself upon this God of mercy. That's the kind of God we need to hear about, even as Christian believers. Even believers who have come to Jesus need to realize the mercy they have in their God.

I like that story of Dr Alexander White who was in Edinburgh at Free St George's for a number of years. This probably happened in the latter part of the nineteenth century. Dr White was going to see one of the men in his congregation, I think he was probably an elder, he was also a lawyer, and he had to go see him on business. He went to the office of Dr John Carmen one day and they took care of their business and then, after all the business was taken care of, Dr Carmen cleared all the papers off his desk and looked at his pastor and said, 'Have ye any word for an old sinner?' This took Dr White aback because he thought John Carmen, who was above 80 years old at the time, was a genuine saint, on the edge of glory, and he didn't know what to say. How often do you have a lawyer lean across his desk and say to you, 'Have ye any word for an old sinner?' So Dr White was nonplussed for a few moments, and then came flooding into his mind the text that he had been using and giving to various people in his pastoral calling that afternoon: Micah 7:18, referring to the Lord where it says, 'he delighteth in mercy.' The next day he got a letter from Dr Carmen saying that he had been going through a period of intense darkness and lack of assurance and that the four words that his pastor had left with him had brought a flood of light into his soul. That never left him till a few days later he entered the land of eternal day.

The chief of sinners says it's true. Remember what Paul says in 1 Timothy 1:12–17. He talks about being a persecutor and a violent man, but notice twice he says 'I received mercy'. That's why, when you get to 1 Timothy 1:17, you see those words 'To the King of ages, immortal, invisible, the only God, be honour and glory forever and ever. Amen.' Paul didn't write 1 Timothy 1:17 there because he had a marginal note by his papyrus, as if to say, 'Put a little religious fluff in here.' It was a response to what he was saying: 'Look what I was as the chief of sinners, but I received mercy.' The God of justice calls you to the cross of Jesus his Son, where judgement has occurred and where mercy is offered still.

Godliness from head to toe

by Jonathan Lamb

Jonathan Lamb

Jonathan Lamb is Director of Langham Preaching for Langham Partnership International, a global programme seeking to encourage a new generation of preachers and teachers. He serves as a Trustee for Keswick Ministries and, following the 2009 Convention, took back the baton of being the Chairman of Keswick Ministries. He regularly speaks at 'Keswicks' in the UK and around the world, and is a member of the preaching team in his local church, St Andrew's, in Oxford. Jonathan is married to Margaret and they have three daughters. He has written several books.

Hands: doing the works of faith: James 2

In week 2 Jonathan Lamb gave five morning Bible expositions on the book of James, under the title 'Godliness from head to toe'. These will be published as a book in the Keswick Study Guides series, but we include one chapter from that series of expositions.

The past twelve months have provided us with many examples in the UK of inconsistency in politics and in the financial sector. The fall-out from the recent problems in Parliament has meant that many people have become cynical about the entire political process. There is an inevitable cynicism, particularly amongst the young, when they see the inconsistency of those who proclaim one thing, but live very differently – whether bankers, politicians, or church leaders. People are weary of 'words' and suspicious of all authority figures. There is an understandable reaction from the man in the street when he sniffs religious humbug, double standards, particularly coming from those who feel they have the right to tell others how they should live.

As Christian believers we know we must set our own house in order. We fear that the way we live often gives the lie to what we preach. In fact, I've often thought that the best phrase is not 'practise what you preach', but 'preach what you practise' – I know it would reduce the number and the length of my sermons. The basic issue we are confronting today was expressed very neatly by John in his first epistle: 'whoever claims to live in him must walk as Jesus did' (1 John 2:6). *Live* like Jesus, don't just *talk* about Jesus. We know that too often this doesn't happen. We can understand E.M. Forster when he described us scornfully: 'Poor talkative little Christianity.'

James chapter 2 is continuing the theme we looked at in chapter 1. We noted that James sees wisdom as not so much to do with intelligence or knowledge, but as a way of life. His letter is calling us to living for Christ wholeheartedly, to live God's way in God's world. As he says in 1:22, 'Do not merely listen to the word, and so deceive yourselves. *Do what it says*' (my italics). And again in 1:25, 'not forgetting what he has heard, but *doing* it – he will be blessed in *what he does*' (my italics). If yesterday we looked at 'Feet: walking the way of wisdom', today we look at 'Hands: doing the works of faith'. We'll look at this chapter in three sections: faith and favouritism; faith and obedience; faith and action.

1. Faith and favouritism 2:1–7

'My brothers, as believers in our glorious Lord Jesus Christ, don't show favouritism' (Jas. 2:1). 'Favouritism': the word here means making judgements or making distinctions between people based on external factors. It is making a judgement about someone's worth based on very superficial criteria. And in verse 4 James says: 'have you not discriminated among yourselves . . .?' We saw in 1:6 that James described the instability of the doubter, the double-minded person. Here in chapter 2 he indicates that to discriminate means to make a distinction: discrimination in the community is another example of a wavering, divided attitude, to which he has referred in chapter 1. James implies, 'The division you are making between rich and poor reflects a divided mind.' We will see this throughout James's letter: discrimination is another example of trying to live in two worlds at the same time, to be friends with the world as well as friends with God.

The story in these verses is instantly recognizable to us because it highlights the importance of 'image' – what people look like. If ever there has been an age which is interested in this theme, it's ours! And we can easily picture what James describes. Someone of considerable status arrives at the congregation, and in verse 2 James gives a colourful description of a person effectively having 'gold fingers'. It was a statement of status as well as wealth – some people rented rings in order to impress others at social occasions. And then verse 2 continues: 'a poor man in shabby clothes also comes in'. James heightens the contrast, because he uses a word for poor which expressed the most severe form of poverty, the person who is destitute.

And how do they respond? They give special attention to the man wearing fine clothes. 'Here's a good seat for you' (v. 3). Sit 'here' implies a special privileged position, near the speaker, near the front, not necessarily so that they could have a good view, but so that others could have a good view of them. And the poor man? 'Stand over there at the back; sit on the floor at my feet. Even better, stand outside in the corridor.'

We know that this kind of discrimination has been a problem throughout the history of the church. Walter Kaiser has pointed out that in the eighteenth century, some churches had become so elitist that John Wesley had to resort to the open fields and graveyards to proclaim the good news to coal miners and the poor.[1] The Methodists opened their doors to all, irrespective of their social standing. Then more than a century later William Booth founded the Salvation Army to do exactly the same. And other independent and informal networks of churches are doing the same today, because it is a recurrent problem.

For some years I worked amongst students in Russia, and made trips to Novosibirsk in Siberia. It was a great joy to see several Art students come to faith. But when I returned some months later, I discovered they had set up a small group as a replacement for a church. I asked them why, and they said that none of the churches they had visited had made them welcome because of the way they dressed. They were poor, of course, not just because they were students but because this was a difficult time in Russia; and their dress may have been more unusual, because they were Art students too. But how sad that churches appeared to exclude young believers on such a basis.

The principle is much wider, of course. James is highlighting a deep concern of the letter, which relates to how we view the poor. He's mentioned this several times already, as we saw in chapter 1: 'The brother in humble circumstances' (1:9); 'orphans and widows' (1:27). How we behave towards one another indicates what we believe about God. Why is favouritism incompatible with true Christian faith? James gives us several reasons, but we will highlight two:

i) Because of Jesus' example 2:1,7

'My brothers, as believers in our glorious Lord Jesus Christ, don't show favouritism' (2:1). Favouritism is inconsistent behaviour for those who believe in Jesus, the Lord of glory. First, if he is our Lord, then this levels each one of us. Jesus is our Lord, we are his servants, and so we are equal. There is absolutely no hierarchy in Christian fellowship – no rich and poor, no male and female, no white and black, no clergy and laity, no young and old. There are no distinctions to be made if Jesus is Lord.

Second, if he is our Lord, then how can we possibly become the judge of others? That's what is happening, James says in verse 4: 'have you not discriminated among yourselves and become judges with evil thoughts?' If you make distinctions between people based on what they look like, you are no longer a Christian brother, you are a judge. And if so, what can you mean when you say Jesus is Lord?

And third, think about how Jesus became 'the Lord of glory' as we could translate verse 1. 'For you know the grace of our Lord Jesus Christ, that though he was rich, yet for your sakes he became poor, so that you through his poverty might become rich' (2 Cor. 8:9). It is totally inconsistent to behave with this kind of favouritism whilst at the same time declaring your belief in our glorious Lord Jesus. Jesus wasn't interested in image. And he was no friend of the religious elite! Social climbers didn't spend a lot of time with him. For many people in his day, he came from the wrong town in the wrong region, he wasn't a graduate of their accepted schools, and he was followed by all the wrong people. But the common people heard him gladly.

I love Mary's song in Luke 1. It underlines what James said in 1:9: 'The brother in humble circumstances ought to take pride in his high position.' Do you remember her words? 'He has brought down rulers from their thrones but has lifted up the humble. He has filled the hungry with good things but has sent the rich away empty' (Luke 1:52,53). Michael Townsend paraphrases James 2:1, 'Are you really trying to combine faith in Jesus Christ, our glorified Lord, with the worship of rank?'[2]

And James makes reference to the Lord Jesus again in this section. Referring to the rich who exploit them and drag them into the courts, he says in verse 7: 'Are they not the ones who are slandering the noble name of him to whom you belong?' The very people you are seeking to honour are the people who oppress and persecute the Christian church. Calvin highlighted the inconsistency when he suggested it was odd to honour one's executioners and in the meantime to ignore one's friends! They slander the name to whom you belong! That's the real issue – not just the injustice of persecution, but that they blaspheme that honourable name by which you are called. You carry the name 'Christian'. You are 'believers in our glorious Lord Jesus Christ' (v. 1). If you carry that name, you must live that life.

Why is favouritism incompatible with true faith? First, because of Jesus' example. Second,

ii) Because of God's call 2:5–7

'Listen . . .' It's an emphatic point – 'listen well'. 'Has not God chosen those who are poor in the eyes of the world to be rich in faith and to inherit the kingdom he promised those who love him? But you have insulted the poor' (vv. 5,6a).

As we have said, how we behave towards one another indicates what we believe about God. So once again James is underlining inconsistency. Think about the people whom God has chosen. Of course, God doesn't show favouritism, selecting a particular class or socio-economic bracket. But he is specially concerned about those whom our society dismisses, or looks down on, or discards. Abraham Lincoln said that 'God must love the common people, because he made so many of them.' And God shows his grace to the humble, the poor, the needy because they are most keenly aware of their own inadequacy. James sustains this refrain: God has a special concern for the poor and helpless. But as James is implying in verse 6, too often the church shows deference to the rich. We have a friend in Côte d'Ivoire who has written on James. He says that in African society the rich are easily noticed and the poor find themselves shoved to one side because, as the proverb says, 'Thin cows are not licked by their friends.' But he also writes: 'God is on the side of the poor, not because they are poor but because they are responsive to him and are near the Kingdom.'[3]

I know that some people object to the language of 'God's bias to the poor.' And they are right that God's arms are outstretched to all. He doesn't show favouritism, as Peter had to learn in the house of Cornelius. But neither is God looking for worthy people. This is what Ronald Sider wrote some years ago: 'By contrast to the way you and I, as well as the comfortable and powerful of every age and society, always act toward the poor, God seems to have an overwhelming bias in favour of the poor. But he is biased only in contrast with our sinful unconcern. It is only when we take our perverse preference for the successful and wealthy as natural and normative that God appears biased.'[4]

As Mary's song reminds us, the powerful and the wealthy and the proud are going to have a tough time. It is the poor, those who know their need of God, who are rich in faith who will inherit the Kingdom. So when Paul commented on the Corinthian church he said: 'Brothers, think of what you were when you were called. Not many of you were wise by human standards; not many were influential; not many were of noble birth' (1 Cor. 1:26, and also 27,28). 'Not many' implies at least some. But such people find it very difficult to lay aside their wealth and privileges. We have a friend who moved from the UK to Vancouver. He is a fine evangelist, but he told us he found it much harder working there because, as he said, 'They think they're in heaven already.' That's the problem for the rich and comfortable. By contrast, the overwhelming majority in the church of God globally come from amongst the poor.

One of the new atheists, who lines up with people like Richard Dawkins and Christopher Hitchens, is Sam Harris. He says some things that we need to listen to carefully. But in one of his recent books, *Letter to a Christian Nation*, he makes a really unfortunate remark. He argues that religion is bad for you, submitting the following evidence.

> Norway, Iceland, Australia, Canada, Sweden, Switzerland, Belgium, Japan, the Netherlands, Denmark and the United Kingdom are among the least

religious on earth. According to the UK Human Development Report (2005) they are also the healthiest, as indicated by life expectancy, adult literacy, per capita income, educational attainment, gender equality, homicide rate, and infant mortality. Insofar as there is a crime problem in western Europe, it is largely the product of immigration. Conversely, the 50 nations now ranked lowest in terms of the United Nations' human development index are unwaveringly religious.[5]

In other words, the least Christian nations are in the north – we are pagans, but healthy and wealthy pagans. The poorest nations, on the other hand, are the most Christian nations. So there's the proof: religion must be bad for you. Leaving aside the glaringly obvious question of the morality of rich western nations which have plundered and exploited the world's poor, Sam Harris needs to meet the Christian believers in these broken and poverty-stricken societies, and compare them with the affluent cynics of our society, before he draws his conclusion about who really is in the healthiest position. There are different kinds of riches and poverty as the risen Christ reminded the church in Laodicea. And hence verse 5: 'Has not God chosen those who are poor . . . to be rich in faith'. David Field is right when he says that, even if a person has no money at all, they are top of God's league table of the world's richest people.

So James gives us good reasons why faith and favouritism cannot belong together. All such discrimination is evil because of these two reasons: Jesus' example and God's call. We now come to the second section of our passage.

2. Faith and obedience 2:8–13

James continues his argument against favouritism by now addressing the theme of obedience to the law.

i) Law and love 2:8–11

'If you really keep the royal law found in Scripture, "Love your neighbour as yourself," you are doing right. But if you show favouritism, you sin and are convicted by the law as law-breakers' (2:8,9).

Here James quotes from Leviticus 19, the royal law to 'love your neighbour as yourself'. He calls it the royal law perhaps because it is this law which rules over all other laws. I will make this point several times: *Paul says the same as James.* On this issue he writes in Romans 13:8–10 that 'he who loves his fellow-man has fulfilled the law'. He lists various commandments, and then says that they 'are summed up in this one rule: "Love your neighbour as yourself"' (quoting Lev. 19 just as James does). 'Love does no harm to its neighbour. Therefore, love is the fulfilment of the law.' The call to love our neighbour means we are to treat everyone, rich and poor, in the same way. We are to love as God loves: no favourites. To discriminate is to decide who is worthy of my love and who is not. So favouritism is a failure of love. James says that faith and obedience to the law belong together. And Paul says the same thing. In talking to the Corinthians about generous giving, he says 'men will praise God for the obedience that accompanies your confession of the gospel of Christ' (2 Cor. 9:13). That's the obedience of faith that James is calling for.

But, you say, surely we are not under law but under grace? True, but again let's listen to Paul in Galatians, that great letter about grace and freedom, 'You, my brothers, were called to be free. But do not use your freedom to indulge the sinful nature; rather, serve one another in love.' And he quotes Leviticus 19: 'The entire law is summed up in a single command: "Love your neighbour as yourself"' (Gal. 5:13,14).

So if you discriminate, you become the moral arbiter, you decide which laws you will obey and which you won't. But verses 10 and 11 show us that God's commands aren't a multiple choice exam paper where you choose any four out of ten. It's no good saying 'I haven't committed adultery', if you fail to care for a needy person – the law is one whole, not separate units. James urges us to see that the whole law is God's will. Faith requires obedience to all that God says. And there is an important encouragement here. 'Speak and act as those are going to be judged by the law that gives freedom' (v. 12).

The law of liberty – 'the perfect law that gives freedom' – was mentioned by James in 1:25 in contrast to the law which only condemns. It is the law that gives freedom. We once had a goldfish in a small bowl in our kitchen. His name was Julian. Just imagine that he wanted to enjoy greater freedom. He could jump out of the bowl on to the kitchen floor, but he wouldn't enjoy freedom. He would go where all good goldfish go. But if he jumped out into a stream or lake, then he would enjoy greater freedom. He would still be living in the environment for which he was created. So it is for humankind. We only discover freedom by living within the parameters which God, the good Creator, has defined. And the Christian experiences fulfilment by living according to his will. We are forgiven and empowered by the Spirit, so we have the freedom to live as we should. We have the power to obey Christ.

I think it was Alec Motyer who told the story of a Japanese Christian who was a thief before he was converted to Christ. After his conversion, he visited a church and saw, written on the wall, the Ten Commandments. And one commandment leapt out at him: 'Thou shalt not steal.' But now he saw it in a new way. Not, 'Thou shalt NOT steal', but 'Thou SHALT not steal.' 'What had formerly been a condemning precept was now a life-giving promise, 'Thou *shalt* not steal.' So in Christ the precepts of the law have become promises to the believer, bringing the liberty of obedience.

ii) Judgment and mercy 2:12, 13

'Speak and act as those who are going to be judged by the law that gives freedom, because judgment without mercy will be shown to anyone who has not been merciful. Mercy triumphs over judgment!' (2:12,13).

Once again James echoes the words of Jesus. We will be judged according to how we have shown mercy. 'Blessed are the merciful, for they will be shown mercy' (Matt. 5:7). Believers too will face judgement. This is not a judgement that determines whether or not we will be saved, for 'there is now no condemnation for those who are in Christ Jesus' (Rom. 8:1). But there is a judgement of our stewardship. It is described in 2 Corinthians 5:10: 'For we must all appear before the judgement seat of Christ, that each one may receive what is due to him for the things done while in the body, whether good or bad.' As Paul teaches in 1 Corinthians 3:10–15, one day the quality of our building work will be tested, and on that judgement day will it survive or will it disappear in a cloud of smoke? How you live your life counts. Have we lived lives worthy of the example and the name of Christ? Have we fulfilled the royal law?

So showing mercy to those in need, which is the sustained argument James gives us, is a necessary sign of true faith and obedience. Showing mercy doesn't win salvation for us, but it is proof of genuine faith, and therefore proof of the reality of our capacity to experience God's mercy. But James brings another pithy saying in verse 13. 'Mercy triumphs over judgment!' As I have mentioned, we need have no fear of condemnation. If God's mercy has embraced us, we are secure. But we can't use this to soften all that James has been urging upon us. Indeed, some think James is referring here not to God's mercy triumphing, but to our acts of mercy which triumph over judgement.

The truth is: God gives us more grace, as we will see in chapter 4. God's mercy to sinners is never-ending. We need not live in a spirit of fear about future judgement. The cross demonstrates the reality of this verse: mercy triumphs over judgement. But at the same time, we must not underestimate our moral obligations. Faith and obedience belong together.

Finally, we come to the third section, which is the clearest call for hands to do the works of faith.

3. Faith and action 2:14–26

'What good is it, my brothers, if a man claims to have faith but has no deeds?' (Jas. 2:14)

James is concerned to show us what true faith looks like. Throughout the chapter he has underlined that genuine faith is faith that works. When we face a situation of need, James suggests, there are three ways of responding. They are: religious words, orthodox belief, or true faith.

i) Religious words 2:15–17

'Suppose a brother or sister is without clothes and daily food. If one of you says to him, "Go, I wish you well; keep warm and well fed" but does nothing about his physical needs, what good is it? In the same way, faith by itself, if it is not accompanied by action, is dead'.

Here is someone full of good advice, but who won't lift a finger. They have a mouthful of religious platitudes, but they do nothing in the face of urgent need. Well, what kind of faith is that? It's spurious, James says. It's no surprise that Jesus said the same about the person who has the religious words but fails to do anything. Do you remember his teaching about the false prophets in Matthew 7? 'Not everyone who says to me, "Lord, Lord," will enter the kingdom of heaven, but only he who does the will of my Father who is in heaven.' You can prophesy in his name, perform miracles, have plenty of pious talk – but without action your faith is useless. That's the first response: religious words. Next we come to the second possible response.

ii) Orthodox belief 2:18–20

In verses 18 and 19 James has a conversation: 'someone will say, "You have faith; I have deeds." Show me your faith without deeds and I will show me my faith by what I do. You believe that there is one God. Good! Even the demons believe that – and shudder.'

The second response is orthodox in terms of belief, but once again it is empty in terms of action. Jewish believers would want to affirm their belief that there is one God. It was basic belief expressed in Deuteronomy 6:4: 'Hear, O Israel: The LORD our God, the LORD is one.' If you believe that, James says, 'Good!' But as has often been pointed out, the merely orthodox believer fails to live by the very next verse, Deuteronomy 6:5, with its call to love God wholeheartedly. In fact, if all they do is to repeat orthodox belief, then they are no better than the demons (v. 19). 'Satan and all his evil hordes are monotheists' as Craig Blomberg puts it.[6] According to Mark, the first person to recognize Jesus as the Son of God was a demon. And at least the demons *do something*, even if only to shudder (v. 19). We know that it is very easy for us Christians to have the correct doctrine but to fail to live the truth: orthodox belief, but no action.

An article appeared in *The Times* recently, entitled 'I don't believe believers really believe'. Jamie Whyte wrote, 'The real test for genuine belief is not what people say, but what they do. To believe something is to be disposed to act upon it. The vast majority of western Christians fail this test.' He goes onto say that whilst religious profession is irritating, 'it is not alarming once you realize it is all just talk.'[7]

We have to listen to such criticisms. Here, James is attacking faith that is merely intellectual, that says and believes the right things, but which is not accompanied by obedience. There are such things as Christian tadpoles: creatures with a huge head and not much else. Martin Luther King once described the persistent schizophrenia of Christians who proudly profess certain principles but who practise the very antithesis of these principles: 'How often our lives are characterized by a high blood pressure of creeds and an anaemia of deeds.'[8]

So James summarises in verse 20 with a pun (in his original writing) on the word 'work'. Faith that fails to act is 'workless'. 'Faith that lacks works does not work.' That kind of faith won't save; it's no faith at all. But there is a third response: not religious words, or orthodox belief, but true faith.

iii) True faith 2:21–26

James now gives some real-life examples to illustrate what faith in action looks like. And he turns to a patriarch and a prostitute. If the great Abraham seems too intimidating as an example, then we can also look at the story of Rahab. Abraham, of course, was the supreme example of faith in Scripture. He was willing to sacrifice his own son, verse 21 tells us. So James says, 'You see that his faith and his actions were working together, and his faith was made complete by what he did' (v. 22). He proved his faith was real because he was willing to obey, to do something. In the same way, Rahab showed the same kind of faith (v. 25). She believed in the God of the Israelites and she acted to welcome the spies. It was sacrificial and risky, like Abraham's actions, but she trusted the Lord more than she did the king of Jericho. So Rahab is found in the list of the heroes of faith in Hebrews 11, and is listed in Jesus' genealogy in Matthew 1:5. That is the point of James' real-life illustration: even Rahab the prostitute was considered righteous! Both Abraham and Rahab had faith in God and expressed that in lives of obedience. Their actions proved that their faith in God was authentic.

Of course, this passage is well known because of the suspicion by some, Luther included, that James and Paul disagreed on the most basic issue of Christian doctrine. So let me briefly comment. First, we would want to underline what Scripture affirms: the Christian faith is not founded on *what we do*, but on *what is done*. 'For it is by grace you have been saved, through faith . . . not by works, so that no-one can boast' (Eph. 2:8,9). Paul asserts this truth in several of his letters. Second, he also teaches that such faith is revealed in actions: 'if I have a faith that can move mountains, but have not love, I am nothing (1 Cor. 13:2). 'The only thing that counts is faith expressing itself through love' (Gal. 5:6). Once again, Paul and James are both affirming the reality of faith in action.

But they are also speaking to different issues in their writing. Paul was concerned to address a situation where people believed that they could be saved through the works of the law. They imagined they could be justified simply by obeying the works of the law, that doing these things made a contribution to being made right with God. That's impossible, says Paul. James was concerned to address a situation where people were not demonstrating the works which flow from being saved by the gospel. That's inconsistent, says James. As John Stott expressed it, 'The two men were given a different ministry but not a different message. They proclaimed the same gospel, but with a different emphasis.'[9]

I like the illustration from Francis Gench: 'Paul is dealing with obstetrics, with how new life begins; James is dealing with pediatrics and geriatrics, with how the Christian life grows, matures and ages.'[10] Or if you like, think of Christian conversion as a doorway. Paul stands before the door, and James after the door. Paul talks about what is needed before you enter, James talks about what is required after you enter. Both Paul and James are concerned about true faith. When Paul uses the words 'by grace you have been saved, *through faith*' (my italics), he means living, genuine faith, which throws itself wholeheartedly on Jesus Christ as Saviour. When James uses the word 'faith' in this chapter, you can see what he is referring to – something dead, bogus, useless. So Calvin harmonizes this with a simple expression: 'faith alone justifies, but faith that justifies is never alone.'

Each of the three examples we have looked at has a statement at its close. First, we've looked at the person with *religious words*: James concludes in verse 17: 'faith by itself, if not accompanied by action, is dead.' Second, we've looked at the person with *orthodox belief.* James concludes with verse 20: 'faith without deeds is useless'. And third, we have looked at *true faith.* And James concludes with verse 26: 'As the body without the spirit is dead, so faith without deeds is dead.' The big issue in this chapter is this: genuine faith proves itself by action.

We explained from James chapter 1 that he is concerned to issue a call for integrity. He wants Christians whose words, character and actions are working together. And it is the same in this chapter: 'Hands – doing the works of faith'. We know that this is the kind of Christian faith that God wants. It is the kind of faith that we want. And it is also the kind of faith that the world around us wants to see. In short, it is to be like Jesus, who was 'mighty in word and deed'. John Wesley had a special concern for the poor and travelled some two hundred and fifty thousand miles and preached some forty thousand sermons. And he declared his purpose in life was to 'lift up Christ before the world, bring him into the dingy corners and dark places of the earth where he is unknown . . . and live so closely with him and in him that others may see that there really is such a person as Jesus, because some being proves it by being like him.'

The Word @ 2.30 p.m.

Marriage as God intended

by Tim Chester

Tim Chester

Tim Chester is a leader in The Crowded House, a family of church-planting networks. He is co-director of the Porterbrook Network and the Northern Training Institute. He is the author of a number of books, including *From Creation to New Creation; Good News to the Poor; The Busy Christian's Guide to Busyness* and *You Can Change the World*. He is also series editor of *The Good Book Guides*. His latest book, *The Ordinary Hero*, is about living the cross and resurrection. Tim is married with two daughters.

Marriage as God intended: Ephesians 5:22–33

Introduction

'Jesus went into Galilee, proclaiming the good news of God. "The time has come," he said. "The kingdom of God is near. Repent and believe the good news!"' That's how the beginning of the ministry of Jesus is described in Mark's Gospel (Mark 1:14). Jesus began his ministry by proclaiming the good news – gospel – and that good news was that the kingdom of God was near. God's kingdom was coming because God's King was coming. Except that the rule of God doesn't sound like good news in our culture, does it? Any kind of rule doesn't sound like good news in our culture! We want to be free. We don't want someone else ruling over us. How can the rule of God be good news? 'You're not the boss of me' – that's a theme in the culture. Surely God's rule is bad news.

Believing the lie

That was the lie of Satan right back in the Garden of Eden. What Satan, the serpent, did was to portray God as a tyrant, holding Adam and Eve back. The serpent portrayed God's rule as tyrannical, oppressive, bad news. But God isn't a tyrant; his rule is a rule of blessing, freedom, love, life, justice, peace, blessing, joy. What's all this got to do with marriage? Everything. What Paul says in Ephesians 5 is that a husband is the head of his wife (v. 23) and then it says, 'wives should submit to their husbands in everything' (v. 24). Immediately we think of patriarchal societies in which men have all the power. We think of inferiority and inequality, and it makes us feel a bit uncomfortable, actually with good reason.

Satan portrayed God's rule as tyrannical and the first man and woman believed that lie. You and I believe that lie: we think God's rule is bad news and so we don't want God to be in charge. But not only do we get God wrong, we also get authority wrong. We push God out of the picture. We take over but we rule, not like God, but in the image of Satan's lie about God; we rule like tyrants. We rule in a way that is self-serving. If some of you men are thinking, 'I like the sound of all this wife submitting stuff,' that just proves my point. You like the sound of it because you're selfish and no wonder women resist that!

An illustration

People today have been raised to value independence above every-thing and the result is that love has become a sign of weakness. God said to the first woman, 'You will desire to control your husband, and he will rule over you' or 'he will dominate you'. The wife resists authority, the husband abuses authority. The Bible is the story of God saying, 'My rule isn't like that.' In fact, to make sure we get the point, God sends his own Son, Jesus, to this world and Jesus says,'. . . [I] did not come to be served, but to serve, and to give . . . [my] life as a ran-som for many' (Matt. 20:28). To make sure we get the point, Jesus, our King, dies in our place on the cross. If you really want to know what God's rule looks like, look to the cross and see your King dying in your place. That's how he rules. See his sacrifice; see him collapse exhausted on the cross, bringing freedom to his people.

What Ephesians 5 says is that your marriage must illustrate God's version of authority and freedom. And, if you're single, the same applies in other areas where we either exercise, or submit to, authority. We are to do that in a way that reflects God's version of authority and freedom. Your marriage must demonstrate the true nature of Christ's relationship with his church, that is the point Paul is making. Marriage was always designed to illustrate God's relationship with his people.

There will be times when you say to your friends, 'God is King, Jesus is Lord, turn from running your own life and trust in Jesus.' As we've seen from Mark 1, that's how Jesus described the good news. But people will think, 'Why is that good news? Why would I want to stop running my life and submit to God?' In that moment, they should be able to look at your marriage and say, 'That's why.' Husbands must exercise their authority through love and care for their wives so that people think, 'It is good news to live under authority when authority is like that.' Wives must submit to their husbands with joy, so that people think, 'Maybe it's good to live under God's authority.'

How it works out

Let me begin to try and spell out what that means. First, let's do a quick digression to 1 Peter 3, and begin to see what it *doesn't* mean. 1 Peter 3:1,2: 'Wives, in the same way' – in the NIV it has 'be submissive' but it's actually 'submit' – 'to your husbands so that, if any of them do not believe the word, they may be won over without words by the behaviour of their wives, when they see the purity and reverence of your lives.' And (v. 6) you are Sarah's daughters 'if you do what is right and do not give way to fear.'

What does it *not* mean? It doesn't mean agreeing with everything your husband says, because the wife of 1 Peter 3 believes that Jesus is Lord and her husband doesn't. Submission doesn't mean never trying to change your husband, because, again, the wife of 1 Peter 3 is trying to convert him through her godly life. Submission doesn't mean a wife gets her spiritual strength from her husband in some ways. The wife of 1 Peter 3 cannot get spiritual strength from her husband, because he's not a believer. Nor does submission mean acting out of fear, for the wife of 1 Peter 3 is told to do what is right without fear. Nor does it mean passivity. The young woman in the Song of Songs is vocal and active; in fact, she takes more initiative than the man does. There's mutual respect and dignity.

Let's think what it means when we talk about submission, headship and love. How does this imaging of God's rule work out in marital relationships? Ephesians 5

> Wives, submit to your husbands as to the Lord. For the husband is the head of the wife as Christ is the head of the church, his body, of which he is the Saviour. Now as the church submits to Christ, so also wives should submit to their husbands in everything. Husbands, love your wives, just as Christ loved the church and gave himself up for her to make her holy, cleansing her by the washing with water through the word (vv. 22–26).

Mutual love and submission

The first thing to say about the submission that is asked of wives and the love that is required of husbands is that it looks very similar. Both mutual love and mutual submission are commended within the wider body of Christ. In chapter 5:2, we're told that we are to 'live a life of love, just as Christ loved us and gave himself up for us'. This is very similar language to that which is commended to husbands. Again, in verse 21, speaking to the body of believers, Paul says, 'Submit to one another out of reverence for Christ.'

So they're very similar – but they're not exactly the same. What is asked of women is not the same as what is asked of men. That is because the relationship is compared to the relationship between Christ and the church, and my relationship with Christ is not a mirror of his relationship to me. Christ does not submit to me.

What does it mean for a wife to submit? What does it mean for a husband to love in the way that Paul describes? I think it means that the wife puts her husband's will before her own and the husband puts his wife's interests before his own. That begins to capture the similarity in the respective attitudes, but also captures the difference in their roles. It gives the husband a lead role, but one defined by the cross; that seeks the good of the other rather than self-interest. And that's even more important, it captures how their respective roles correspond to the roles of the church towards Christ, and Christ towards the church. The church puts Christ's will before its own; Christ puts the church's interest before his own.

One believer to another

People sometimes say that 'Submit to one another out of reverence for Christ' (v. 21) is a kind of heading for this section. I don't think that's quite right. I think there is an important truth there; it is appropriate for a husband to submit to his wife as one believer to another. It's not difficult to see the circumstances in which that might operate. A wife might say to her husband, 'I hope you don't mind my mentioning it, but the way you spoke to Jack was not really consistent with someone who claims to belong to Christ.' A godly husband might say, 'You're right. Thank you for loving me enough to challenge me.' There is an appropriateness about a husband submitting to his wife as one believer to another. But 'Submit to one another' is not the heading for the section on marriage. It's actually the climax of the previous section. What Paul says there is that we are to be filled with the Spirit, and then he gives four sub-clauses that spell out what that means.

Men and women are equal but equality doesn't rule out complementary roles or headship, otherwise we can't have a proper doctrine of the Trinity. The Persons of the Trinity are equal in terms of their being, their Godness, if you like, but the Son puts himself under the authority of the Father; he puts the Father's will before his own. That's the point Paul makes in 1 Corinthians 11:3: 'Now I want you to realise that the head of every man is Christ, and the head of the woman is man, and the head of Christ is God.'

Consider how we submit to political authorities or employers. If a policeman flags you down and taps on the window, you submit to him. You don't think that he is a superior person in terms of his humanity, but you know that, in that moment, he is playing the role of someone who is in authority and you submit to that. I think that is true of what's going on here; it's not that women are less equal, but that God has set it up in this way so that the wife puts the husband's will before her own and the husband puts his wife's interests before his own. Some people stress the reciprocal nature of this, almost to the point where the wife submits to the husband to the extent that the husband loves her as Christ loves the church; or some people stress the 'in everything' (v. 24) – the wife submits to her husband in everything, almost to the extent that if the husband is abusive, still the wife submits. I don't think it's helpful to push it to those extremes, but we must submit even when our spouse is not perfect, otherwise there would be no submission and no love. There would just be this vicious cycle of recrimination: 'I'll submit to you when you love me.' 'I'll love you when you submit to me.' And you just grow further and further apart.

Neither submission nor love are weak or passive. They should be robust and reinforced by gospel convictions. We should challenge one another; speak the truth in love to one another, as Paul says in chapter 4. But the point is this: we do not do this for our sake; we do this for the sake of Christ and his glory, and for the sake of our spouse and their holiness.

Submitting to Christ

Let me come back to those statements that I made about what it means. It means the wife puts her husband's will before her own and the husband puts his wife's interests before his own. Let me highlight what that *doesn't* say. It doesn't mean that the wife puts her husband's will first and it doesn't mean that the husband puts his wife's interests first. They put each other's will or interests before their own, but not first! The first place belongs to Christ. Both of them have a higher allegiance and a higher purpose, to submit to Christ and seek his glory. And that means there will be times when the wife challenges her husband, there will be times when she rejects her husband's will, in order to be obedient to Christ's will.

There is one important difference between submitting to a husband and submitting to Christ. Your husband is not God and he will make mistakes, he will make bad judgements, and sometimes you will need to challenge him because your top allegiance is to Christ. You are to speak the truth in love to him. There will be times when a husband puts his wife's holiness before her happiness. He's seeking her interests, not just whatever she wants. I could refine my formula by saying the wife puts her husband's will before her own but not before Christ's will, and the husband puts his wife's interests before his own but not before Christ's interests.

I hardly need point out to you that this biblical teaching runs contrary to the spirit of our age, but the answer is not to make the Bible conform to our world-view but to make our world-view conform to that of the Bible, to be counter-cultural. God's rule is liberating and life-giving and loving.

Wives

The wife submits by putting her husband's will before her own. The first thing that means is that the wife must submit to her husband and not to others. I wonder if that is the force of what Paul says: 'Wives, submit to your husbands as to the Lord' (v. 22). When you get married, there's a change of allegiance. In the day when Paul was writing, the wife lived under the authority of her father but when she married, that relationship changed. Her primary allegiance was now to her husband.

In our day, it's different. More often than not, a woman has left home and has lived on her own as a single woman. Women live under their own authority, making decisions for themselves. God is saying, in effect, 'Wives, submit to your husbands instead of just submitting to yourselves.' You have to bear in mind the fact that you are now married, you now have a new allegiance.

Freedom

It means submitting without whining – would that illustrate how the church should relate to Christ? We are to submit joyfully. Paul's joy in God is like the air that inflates this letter and it keeps bursting out. The letter begins with him saying, 'Praise be to the God and Father of our Lord Jesus Christ, who has blessed us in the heavenly realms with every spiritual blessing' (Eph. 1:3). And he keeps talking about God's incomparable riches: Ephesians 1:18,19; 2:7; 3:8,16. Again and again, it keeps coming out. And in chapter 5 verses 19 and 20: 'Sing and make music in your heart to the Lord, always giving thanks to God the Father for everything'. That is how we are to submit to the authority of Christ, with a song in our hearts, and that is how wives are to submit to their husbands.

It means also submitting without manipulating. I have met women who loudly affirm headship and submission but, in practice, have manipulated their husbands. In fact, I remember a woman saying, 'Ahh, headship, authority . . . don't worry, ladies, we know how to get our own way.' Does that illustrate how the church submits to Christ? Of course not; Christ is not a henpecked husband who does our bidding. We submit to him as God's Son and God's King. Above all, submission means submitting freely and willingly.

People have often observed the similarities between what Paul teaches here and Greek ethical teachings in the secular morality of the day. There are some very striking similarities, but several differences, and one really important difference is that Greek ethical instruction was never addressed to women. The husband was told to make his wife submit, but that is not what Paul says because he assumes that women are free and equal in God's kingdom, and then he asks them to submit freely and willingly to the authority of their husbands.

Wives must model the freedom of submission. We don't *lose* our freedom when we submit to the authority of God. We *find* our freedom. We discover that his rule is a rule of life and blessing and freedom and joy. We are set free from the slavery to other people, their opinions, our own sinful desires, the rule of Satan, and instead we become free to be the people we should be.

Husbands

The husband loves by putting his wife's interests before his own. What does that mean? Verse 25: 'love your wives, just as Christ loved the church and gave himself up for her.' What is Christ's rule over his church like? What does his authority look like? The answer is love.

Christ loved the church and what does that look like? It looks like the cross. His rule is sacrificial, serving and selfless.

'Husbands, love your wives, just as Christ loved the church and gave himself up for her to make her holy, cleansing her by the washing with water through the word, and to present her to himself as a radiant church, without stain or wrinkle or any other blemish, but holy and blameless' (vv. 25–27). Every bride looks beautiful as she walks down the aisle on her wedding day, but what about first thing in the morning? When Christ looks at me, he looks past my exterior and sees my heart and what he sees is very, very ugly. People often put up pictures of their wedding day around their homes. Imagine instead a picture of your heart on the wall for everyone to see, a picture of all the things you have ever done and said and thought on display. Are you brave enough to look beyond the exterior and look at your ugly heart?

Christ sees us, and he loves us and he makes us his. And that's why he died; it wasn't a kind of mad romantic gesture. He took our stain, our ugliness, our corruption, on himself. He died the death we deserve in our place and then, three days later, he rose again to give us life. He died for us and he lives for us. Our ugliness was transferred on him, on the cross, when he died, and his goodness was transferred on us when we believe in him, so we end up being holy and blameless. And that is how, husbands, you are to treat your wife; you are to love her in a sacrificial, selfless way; you are to give yourself up for her. You are to give yourself for her and then you are to give yourself for her again – and again.

Agenda

I want you to notice this: Christ loves us unconditionally but he loves us with an agenda. He loves us because he loves us. There's nothing in us that draws out his love. Paul has said, 'For it is by grace you have been saved, through faith – and this not from yourselves, it is the gift of God – not by works, so that no-one can boast' (Eph. 2:8,9). There were no works that we did that drew his love. He loved us simply because he loved us, because of his grace. Christ did not make us his bride because of the good works we had done. He made us his bride because of his love and his grace. He loves us unconditionally but he loves us with an agenda, and that agenda is to make us holy and blameless. He has an agenda of change. Christ does not love us *because* of anything other than his grace but he does love us *for* something: to make us holy and radiant.

Husbands, that's how you are to love your wives; unconditionally but with an agenda. So you don't just love her when she's looking beautiful or when she's treating you well, you're to love her all the time – but you should have an agenda, and that agenda is the same as Christ's agenda: to make her holy and blameless, to help her grow as a Christian, to help her become more like the Lord Jesus. You are to love her as Christ loved the church.

Christ gave up everything for us; he put our relationship with God before his relationship with God. On the cross he cried, 'My God, my God, why have you forsaken me?' (Matt. 27:46). He experienced the end of his relationship with God that we might enter into a relationship with God. He put our needs before his needs. And that's the standard for husbands: you are to give up everything for your wife, to put her relationship with God even before your own, to put her needs before your needs.

We start marriage full of good intentions to serve her selflessly. But she isn't always radiant. Some days she will be grumpy or annoying or withdrawn, but remember, Christ didn't love us because we *were* radiant, but to *make* us radiant. Perhaps the bigger problem is, not that there are days when your wife is tired and grumpy, but there are days when *you* are tired and grumpy. Those are the days when I find it hard to love my wife: when I'm feeling low, when I'm struggling. Yet still you must go on giving yourself to her, no exceptions.

I think that's why the passage goes on in the way that it does. 'In this same way, husbands ought to love their wives as their own bodies' (v. 28). You get home and all you want to do is put your feet up and chill out in front of the telly. But that is how you are to love your wife and so you say, 'I'll do the washing up.' Care for her like you care for yourself. Most men are quite good at knowing what it means to love themselves; you've just got to learn to love your wife in that way. If you love your wife selflessly, sacrificially, serve well in the insignificant and distasteful things of life, then you will show people the good news of Jesus. They will see that it is good to live under God's authority.

Leadership

One area where I've been convicted in recent years is this area. I'm not being a servant-leader in my marriage if I say 'whatever'. I don't know how the dynamics work in your life and your marriage, but this is how Saturdays and holidays work in the Chester household. I'm often up first and I'm in my study pottering around. It takes a while for the rest of the family to get up and then, at some point, my wife takes the initiative for some family activity and I acquiesce, often reluctantly, because I quite like pottering around in my study. I acquiesce because I want to serve my wife, but I do so passively. And, of course, my wife senses that my heart isn't in it. I have put her interests before my own but only in a formal passive sense. I haven't led in that situation. So what should I do?

I should take some leadership. That doesn't mean that I decide what we're going to do and then drag her along reluctantly. That would be to lord it over my family. Instead it means coming up with a plan that I think will please my wife. It might mean surprising her; it doesn't have to be anything elaborate or extravagant, just some proactive plan to put her interests before my own, to bless her.

So you're not being a good husband when you proactively pursue your interests but nor, I think, when you passively acquiesce to your wife's interests. You're being a good husband when you proactively pursue your wife's interests. For some, the temptation or tendency is to be domineering, lording it over your wife, proactively pursuing your own interests. But there may be others who acquiesce and think we're putting her first, but we're passive. You're being a good husband when you proactively pursue your wife's interests.

I find it helpful to think of it like this: the husband has the responsibility of taking the initiative within the marriage. That doesn't mean that the wife can be irresponsible, nor that she can never take the initiative, but the husband has the responsibility of taking the initiative. If there's a conflict in their marriage, then he has the responsibility to take the initiative to resolve the conflict. If a decision has to be made, he has the responsibility to ensure the decision is made in a godly way. When it comes to raising children, he has the responsibility to ensure they are disciplined and taught. That doesn't mean he's going to do it all, but neither is he going to abdicate responsibility to his wife – he must take the initiative.

I think, in our culture, we have two contrasting models of what it means to be male, and neither of them is biblical. First of all there is Domineering Dominic. Domineering Dominic thinks to be manly is to be muscled, arrogant, macho, aggressive. Family revolves around him, everyone else must fit in with him, he has his chair, he has his timetable, he has his taste to which everyone else must conform. And I think sometimes some Christians do a version of that; they bulk up to be manly, they glorify aggression. Domineering Dominic takes the initiative, but only to pursue his own interests.

On the other hand, there is Passive Patrick, who's very much in touch with his feminine side, influenced by the version of feminism that downplays the differences between men and women. He never takes the initiative because he doesn't want to offend his right-on friends. And there's another version – Passive Patrick: the Grown-up Kid. This is the *Men Behaving Badly* man; boys with their toys; one of the lads, up for a laugh. Maybe that's appropriate when you're fifteen, but not when you're twenty-five, and not when you're married. That is not what it means to be manly. Some men need to grow up. You think you're being manly, but you're just a posturing adolescent.

Domineering Dominic, Passive Patrick are the two options, I think, that are offered by our culture. But they're not our only options and they're not the biblical option. To be manly is to accept responsibility by taking the initiative; not just in marriage, actually, but in the wider community, in the church, in the home, in the workplace, in all these areas. To be truly manly is to take responsibility. The man who works long hours in a dead-end job to provide for his family and then, when he comes home, sees his wife tired from looking after the children, so he offers to wash up and bath the children, he's being manly. That's a man I can admire.

A godly man takes the initiative; he takes responsibility in the home, in the church, in the community. He takes the initiative to put out the chairs, to pray in the prayer meetings, to talk to the newcomers, to resolve conflict, to volunteer in the community, to check on an elderly neighbour. Someone who takes responsibility, that's what it means to be manly, in biblical terms.

Shalom

Let me highlight this encouragement. Chapter 5:18: 'Instead, be filled with the Spirit.' God has set you a high standard; you are to illustrate his relationship to the church; you are to make his good news known through your marriage. I think it's a particularly high standard for men because our standard is the cross of Jesus, but God also gives you his Spirit. God has given you himself. God himself has given you a new desire and a new power to live right.

Earlier on in Ephesians Paul prays, 'I pray that out of his glorious riches he may strengthen you with power through his Spirit in your inner being, so that Christ may dwell in your hearts through faith' (3:16,17). Let me suggest to you that as you read these verses on marriage, you need to be praying that prayer, because of the challenge they put before us.

So this modelling of Christ's relationship to his church, through submission and love, is the way of the Spirit, but it's also the way of blessing. Putting someone's will before your own, or putting someone's interests before your own, doesn't sound like much fun but it is the way of blessing and it is the way to find life. Jesus said, 'If anyone wants to be my follower, you must turn from your selfish ways, take up your cross and follow me. If you try to hang on to your life, you will lose it, but if you give up your life for my sake and for the sake of the good news, you will save it.' Marriage is one of the powerful ways in which we can show people that giving up your life is the way to gain life. In marriage we learn that we find our lives by giving up our lives. I give away the freedoms of a single man but I gain the greater joys of covenant love. I find the restrictions of marriage in fact enable me to be free, if that's what God calls me to.

In the Song of Songs, the lover calls his beloved 'my shalomite girl'. It's not that she's from this place Shalom, it's probably his girl of *shalom*: peace and completeness. She gives him rest and makes him complete. One of the refrains of the Song of Songs is 'My lover is mine and I am his.' It's the language of ownership, of possession. You give yourself away and belong to another, but it is mutual possession and mutual belonging. In marriage, I learn to enjoy belonging to another. Through marriage, we learn what a delight it can be to say, 'My Jesus is mine, and I am his. He is Lord, he is my Lord. I belong to him.' We rejoice to hear God saying again and again, through the Bible story, 'I will be your God, and you will be my people.'

I discover, through marriage, how serving someone else brings me pleasure. It's so tragic when couples are trying to get the most from each other. They may be people who never have a full-blown argument, but there's a kind of constant competition going on; all responsibilities are negotiated. One party serves the other perhaps out of fear, or because getting the other one to help is more trouble than it's worth. Who does the washing up? Is it always the same person? Is it manipulated? Is it negotiated? Or is there joy in serving the other by washing up?

Nowhere is this more true than in sex. In sex you get pleasure by giving pleasure. Sex teaches us the pleasure of self-giving, the pleasure of giving pleasure, the love of loving, the honour of honouring, the blessing of being a blessing. You find pleasure in sex by giving pleasure. And so marriage and sex teach us that love is its own reward, that joy is found in service, that it is more blessed to give than to receive, that you gain your life by giving up your life. When men take responsibility, when they give their lives, they discover their lives. Let me end with that challenge, that in marriage, let's rise to that challenge of illustrating Christ's love to his church, and the liberating rule of God in our lives – that God's kingdom is good news.

The Lecture

Week 1: Christianity in a collapsing culture

by Lyndon Bowring

Lyndon Bowring

Lyndon Bowring has been executive Chairman of CARE for over twenty-five years. He was born in Wales, studied at London Bible College and was a full-time minister at Kensington Temple for ten years. He is now a 'consultant minister' at the church, and is on the board or Council of Reference for many Christian organizations, and speaks regularly at Christian events. Lyndon loves London and lives there with his wife, Celia, a writer and speaker. They have three children: Daniel, Emma and Andrew. Lyndon's hobbies include cooking, watching rugby, building friendships and exploring London.

Christianity in a collapsing culture

Jesus said: You are the salt of the earth. But if the salt loses its saltiness, how can it be made salty again? It is no longer good for anything, except to be thrown out and trampled by men. You are the light of the world. A city on a hill cannot be hidden. Neither do people light a lamp and put it under a bowl. Instead they put it on its stand, and it gives light to everyone in the house. In the same way, let your light shine before men, that they may see your good deeds and praise your Father in   heaven' (Matt. 5:13–16).

I want to talk firstly about the uniqueness of Christianity, and then about the meaning of culture. Thirdly, I want to talk about the collapse of our culture, and then lastly, and most importantly, our Christian response – how should we live in the light of this great unique gospel of our Lord Jesus Christ?

The uniqueness of Christianity

A group of theologians were trying to summarize the uniqueness of Christianity, and who should come into the room but the esteemed professor C.S. Lewis, the Christian apologist. They said, 'Professor Lewis, we're trying to summarize Christianity in as few words as possible. Help us.' The professor said, 'I'll give it to you in one word.'

Can you imagine? We can summarize the whole of the Christian gospel, its uniqueness, in one word. And this one word is not in any other religion – it's unique to Christianity. It's that word 'grace'.

Salvation is through grace, by grace; through faith, by faith. We are justified by faith, by what Jesus Christ has done on the cross – he bore in his body the punishment for our sin. He took the wrath of God in our place, that we might in turn receive the righteousness of God. In theological terms it's called 'received righteousness'. God takes our filthy rags and clothes us in the righteousness of Christ.

No other religion in the world is remotely interested in this concept of 'Nothing that I can do, it's all that he has done'; every other religion is about what *they* do, what they attain, what *they* try and so on. But Christianity is about receiving, and the truth is that God showed his love towards us while we were yet sinners. He didn't wait for us to get our act together, sort ourselves out; he came to us in our rebellion, and died for us. Christianity is the only religion whose founder died and yet is still alive today. One of the reasons he went back to the Father was that he could be in a million places at the same time. While he was on earth he was never in more than one place at one time. Now he's wherever two or three are gathered in his name.

Christianity offers total forgiveness for all our sins and the assurance of a place in eternity with God; absolute assurance, not because of what we have done, but because of what Christ has done. No other religion offers that certainty. This God of love, God *is* love, is absent in all other religions. It's unique to Christianity.

The largest movement

Also, the Christian church is the largest movement known to humankind. We're the only organization that never loses a member through death – they haven't died, they've departed. And Paul says in the light of this huge cloud of witnesses there in the heavenlies, we should 'throw off everything that hinders and the sin that so easily entangles, and . . . run with perseverance the race' (Heb. 12:1). And we honour today the departed, those who led us and discipled us and pastored us and cared for us who've gone on to glory. Yes, they've departed, but they're very much alive, and one day we'll join them in that great Millennium Stadium of glory.

So rejoice – whether it's in your worship, whether it's in your quiet time, whether it's in your singing or whether it's in your witness. Don't be ashamed of the uniqueness of the gospel; don't be ashamed that Jesus said, 'I am the way and the truth and the life. No one comes to the Father except through me' (John 14:6).

The meaning of culture

What do we mean by culture? One dictionary definition says, 'The attitudes and values that inform a society' and the late Raymond Johnson described it like this for me: it's 'the essential part of all human social existence . . . a persisting pattern of thinking, feeling, believing and evaluating'. So it's an essential part of all social existence.

The culture of nations is different. We have a certain British culture. Christianity came in the second century AD; it was that great Celtic move throughout the nation. Then came the Church of Rome right across western Europe, and the Orthodox Church to the east of Europe. So Europe became Christendom, unique to this part of God's world. Then came the great Reformation and, with the help of Henry VIII, there was that turning to a Protestant religion that was based on Scripture; Calvin and Luther and so many of those great men brought to us a clear understanding of Scripture. And since then we've had the Protestant church growing in Britain, in Europe and throughout the world. Our country, our laws, our traditions in western Europe are built upon the Bible, upon a Judeo-Christian heritage. But the foundation is crumbling and the question to ask ourselves is, how much of that are we to blame for that erosion?

Drawing them in

We have a culture that is a pattern of our thinking, feeling, believing and evaluating. Therefore, when British people are asked what their religion is, 70 per cent tick the Christian box. It doesn't mean they understand what Christianity is or that they believe the Christian gospel or that they're committed – they may be unbelievers, but Christianity sounds right: 'We're not Muslim, we're not Hindu, we're not Buddhist, we're Christian.' One can be sad and think, 'Isn't it awful that only 5 to 10 per cent will be in church on Sunday' and bemoan that fact, but I think it's something to give thanks to God for. In our evangelism and in our reaching out in the community, we should build on this heritage, not despise or undermine it. Many people are nearer the faith than we realize.

Sometimes in our evangelism, it's 'kingdom of darkness, kingdom of light', but people are on journeys, and many are close to the kingdom. Sometimes we are in danger of unnecessarily alienating them rather than talking to them about this faith which they think they know, and tenderly, gently, drawing them into the kingdom.

So we should build on our Christian heritage, and believe that many people are just there on the cusp, waiting to be lovingly drawn in to the fullness of God's kingdom.

Collapse of our culture

Where did this British post-Victorian culture begin to collapse and crumble? Probably after the First World War; the war that was meant to end all wars. At the same time, Darwin and the fruits of the Enlightenment were gripping our society. The church – which had been an advancing church in the Victorian era, where it made an impact and went out into society – suddenly started to retreat. We began to be preoccupied with our theology, our view of Scripture, the fundamentals. The church was shrinking, handing over the light and salt element to the liberals, and the social gospel came into existence. And so we began to see this gradual retreat – 'We're in the world but not of the world': '. . . come out from them and be separate, says the Lord. Touch no unclean thing . . .' (2 Cor. 6:17). Then there was a Second World War. The church was being gently depleted. And then we came to the 1960s.

In 1979 I was attending the House of Commons when Michael Alison, a godly MP, personal Private Secretary to the Prime Minister, was introducing a Motion. Birmingham City Council Education Committee had decided to abolish RE and schools assemblies in the education curriculum throughout the whole of Birmingham. Michael

Alison realized if he could introduce a Motion and get the majority to vote in favour of it, it would scupper the atheistic humanistic efforts by the Birmingham City Council Education Committee. So, his Motion was 'This House (of Commons) believes that we should maintain and improve RE and schools assemblies throughout the United Kingdom.'

While I was there, standing in the central lobby of the Commons, a member of the House of Lords said to me, 'Lyndon, whilst Christians were asleep in the 1960s, lights went out in this House that may never be relit again.' Great things had been happening in the church and for the church, but most Christians had not even been aware of the debates. They weren't praying and fasting, weren't crying out to God to have mercy. Laws were being repealed; the Witchcraft Act, the Theatres Act; laws relating to abortion, divorce and human sexuality. There was an agenda to erase any legislation that had a remote link to Christianity or the Bible. These endeavours have altered the culture of Britain and we're living with the fruit and the damage – it's called secularization; anti-Christian, anti-Christ, anti-God, anti-Bible. Secularization wants to push Christianity to the margins of our society, to become a private affair within our church walls and in our minds. There ultimately comes a hostility, an anger towards Christianity, anger against the church, that we should think we should have any impact on our society or influence in the institutions of our national life. It was Lesslie Newbiggin, that outstanding thinker and servant of the Lord, who said that the public/private divide – which is what secularization wants; to privately go to church, privately think, privately read, privately have Bible studies, privately pray, privately sing – 'is the most corrosive characteristic of western culture for the life of faith.'

The church, filled with grace and truth, needs to go to and reclaim those areas of society that we have surrendered, where we have retreated and the enemy has advanced. Secularization has swept in like a flood. We need to go in Christ's name and see the Spirit of the Lord raise up a standard against that flood tide and see God's kingdom, by his grace and the leading of his Holy Spirit, advance – enemy territory occupied, lives saved and changed, becoming new lights and fresh salt in our dark and decaying society.

The sanctity of human life

Abortion

I could home in on any one or more moral issues here, but I have chosen to concentrate on the sanctity of human life. In 1967 the Abortion Act was passed, since when millions upon millions of unborn children have been stolen from the womb. (To anyone who may have suffered an abortion – please don't feel condemned; the enemy condemns, God forgives, God heals. That's the God of grace we serve.) The womb is meant to be the most hallowed and safe place. It is where our Lord Jesus Christ chose to live for nine months of his life. He didn't arrive on the stage of our world in a crib, he arrived in the womb of the Virgin Mary. And it was John the Baptist, in the womb of Elizabeth, who was the first human being to recognize – apart from his mother and father – the presence of the only begotten Son of God there in Mary's womb. But in the United Kingdom, the womb, which was to be the safest and most sacred place to live, has become the most dangerous place to live.

Experimentation

If that isn't enough, in 1990 our British parliament voted to permit the experimentation on human embryos. You could take an ovum and sperm, join it in a laboratory and experiment on it for fourteen days and then discard it. Charles Haddon Spurgeon believed that every conceived embryo, when destroyed, or dead through miscarriage or infant mortality after birth, would go straight into the presence of God. Many great orthodox evangelical theologians agree with Spurgeon. If that's the case, there'll be more inhabitants in heaven who never saw the light of day than all those saints of all the ages that were gloriously saved and who lived on earth. In France, if you are caught experimenting on a human embryo, you're given a seven-year prison sentence. In Germany, you're given a five-year prison sentence. Last year the British Parliament approved the creation of animal-human hybrids – taking an animal ovum and linking it with human sperm; taking a human egg and fertilizing it with animal sperm. That is permitted and is currently taking place in research centres throughout our country, for up to fourteen days. In 2005, the then Prime Minister Tony Blair said that he wanted Britain to be the bio-technical capital of the world, and more than one hundred million pounds were set aside for this whole issue of animal–human hybrids, embryonic stem cell research. However, throughout the world, research centres which are not experimenting on embryonic stem cells but instead on adult stem cells have discovered nearly eighty therapies, by taking adult stem cells, cultivating them and putting them back in the body. This is totally ethical, exciting, fantastic, liberating. There are currently a further 350 clinical trials going on to see what other cures we can find by harnessing all the healing propensities that God has put in our bodies.

Euthanasia

I read in one newspaper recently of a couple who went to Dignitas in Switzerland and both took lethal barbiturates and committed suicide together. The wife was terminally ill, and the husband was frail, but not dying. We give thanks to God that Lord Falconer and Baroness Jay were defeated in the House of Lords by fifty-three votes. They wanted to encourage parents, friends and family to be allowed to take people to commit suicide; they wanted to assist people to die. The House of Lords wonderfully rejected the proposal. Holland has euthanasia laws; the majority of older people when polled recently said they were frightened if they were required to go into hospital because there are thousands of recorded involuntary euthanasias that take place in that country. And there is little or no hospice care anywhere to be found in the Netherlands. Britain, starting with Dame Cicely Saunders, is at the forefront of palliative care; we have the greatest palliative care of any country in the world. Life is sacred from birth, from conception, to its natural end.

The Christian response

I was proud, just a couple of years ago, to be in Westminster Abbey, packed to the doors with people remembering Dame Cicely

Saunders' great life. I went down to St Christopher's Hospice in Sydenham, the first hospice in the world, that she had established, and as I walked through the doors you could literally feel the presence of the angels of God, caring for these dying people. That's the Christian response.

Taking risks

The Christian response does *not* include a fortress mentality, this sense of being embattled in this fortress, retreating, just keeping our heads down waiting for the second coming. I sometimes wonder if maybe God, in his sovereignty, will choose not to wind up the affairs of this world for 1,000 years, or 500 years, or 200 years; we'll all have departed and what will be the legacy that we leave behind for our children, grandchildren and great-grandchildren? Wherever you are in the game of life, the journey, I want to urge you today in Christ's name, take risks. Step out in faith.

Prayer

We wonder what's happening in our culture. It was recently reported that a National Health Service leaflet was advising school pupils that regular sexual intercourse could be good for their health and that they had a right to an enjoyable sex life. Young people should be protec-ted and cared for, nurtured and cherished! If you know of young people who are reaching out to other young people, get behind them, pray for them. You may not like the way they're doing it, you might not like the culture that's being imbibed in that kind of loud music or dance, but if young people are reaching out to their peers, they need your grey-haired support. They need your finances. They need the knowledge that you're praying for them every day.

We can all pray, and 1 Timothy 2 urges us to pray for those in authority. We can pray for our evangelists, pray for our young people, pray for those who are out on a mission field. Keswick has got a great missionary tradition. Whether it's abroad or at home, whether it's young, middle-aged or older, let's be prayerful like never before.

Raising up leaders

I meet more and more church leaders who are seeking to proclaim the eternal truths of the word of God as it relates to the sanctity of human life (whether it's the unborn child, the newly born, the handicapped, those towards the end of life), marriage and the family, and a biblical view of sexuality that's good not just for Christians but for the whole of society and I want to commend these pastors and leaders.

CARE has this amazing leadership programme. We take fifteen to twenty young Christian graduates, we put them with MPs for three days a week, and we have them for one day a week. We equip them with a Christian world-view, and see them springboard into significant positions of leadership. Almost two hundred young people have gone through this CARE leadership or internship programme.

During the last election I got a little A5 House of Commons-headed note: 'Dear Lyndon, I came on your intern programme ten years ago. I had a vision to become a Member of Parliament. I'm now in the House. I'm the youngest MP in the House with the smallest majority. Please can we have lunch?' Wonderful!

In the 1780s when William Wilberforce went abroad on his continental holiday with his old Cambridge tutor, Isaac Milner, to read and relax and have a good philosophical discussion about various books, he didn't realize what an evangelical Christian Milner was. Milner led William Wilberforce to Christ. He came home, went straight to see John Newton who was vicar of St Mary's Woolnoth in the city of London, and he said, 'Sir, I have had an evangelical conversion and I'm going into the Anglican ministry.' John Newton said, 'Oh no, you're not! Young man, you have been called to the kingdom for such a time as this.' William Wilberforce thought the highest thing he could do was to go into the ministry. For thirty years he campaigned; he had a nervous breakdown and great ill-health but finally in 1807 the British Parliament voted in favour of the abolition of the slave trade. And it was the first and only time in the history of the House of Commons that the whole House stood and gave a standing ovation.

CARE is working on our leadership programme to see young Wilberforces raised up. We've got interns going in regularly to the BBC, most of whom are now in full-time salaried positions, being salt and light, permeating our society: culture changers, not captivated by our culture.

Light and salt

Robert Bellah, the famous eminent US sociologist said, 'The quality of a culture may be changed when 2 per cent of its people have a new vision.' Two per cent! That's all it would take to change our culture towards God and away from this demonization and secularization that's destroying and damaging so many people. The power of the Christian church to be light and salt . . . John Stott said

> In Britain today there is growing dishonesty, corruption, immorality, violence, pornography, a diminishing respect for human life, and an increase in abortion. Whose fault is it? Let me put it like this: if the house is dark at night, there is no sense in blaming the house. That's what happens when the sun goes down. The question to ask is, 'Where is the light?' If meat goes bad, there is no sense in blaming the meat. That is what happens when the bacteria are allowed to breed unchecked. The question to ask is, 'Where is the salt?' If society becomes corrupt like a dark night or stinking fish, there's no sense in blaming society. That's what happens when fallen human society is left to itself and human evil is unrestrained and unchecked. The question to ask is, 'Where is the church?'

Bill Hybels said recently

> The local church has been entrusted with carrying the life-changing message of Jesus Christ, and it's the only hope I see for this hurting and broken world . . . When the local church is working right, people of faith help bear the burden of those who have nowhere else to turn. Lost people get found, lonely people find community, the bereaved find comfort, thecommitted grow deeper and stronger in their faith.

An Evangelical Alliance report from October 2006 said

> When Christians, motivated by their faith, get involved in their com-
> munity – especially through community-based projects – to work for
> justice, healing and human well-being, they may also be considered to be
> engaged in work for the kingdom . . . The personal ministry of leading
> other individuals to Christ of course remains indispensable, but also
> overall strategies for bringing the transforming power of the gospel to
> bear on the life of the nation, backed by vision involving the possibility
> of societal transformation across the widest possible front, is necessary.

In Isaiah 58, God said: 'day after day they seek me out; they seem eager
to know my ways . . . They ask me for just decisions and seem eager
for God to come near them. "Why have we fasted," they say, "and you
have not seen it? Why have we humbled ourselves, and you have not
noticed?"' (vv. 2,3). So here were a people who were fasting and praying and seeking the face of God. God said, 'the kind of fast I have chosen . . . [is] to loose the chains of injustice and untie the cords of the
yoke, to set the oppressed free and break every yoke' (vv. 5,6). Sharing
food with the hungry, providing the poor wanderer with shelter, seeing the naked and clothing them – that's what God was looking for.

We must pray, and pray more. But prayer is not enough; we've got
to get up off our knees and out of the four walls of the church, beyond
the ministries that are there for our edification and our building up
and information, and reach out into the community, in Christ's name,
to be salt and light, permeating, penetrating, proclaiming, caring. And
if we do, this is what God says

> Then your light will break forth like the dawn . . . your healing will
> quickly appear . . . your righteousness will go before you, and the glory
> of the LORD will be your rear guard. Then you will call, and the LORD
> will answer; you will cry . . . and he will say: Here am I. . . . then your
> light will rise in the darkness . . . your night will become like the noon-
> day. The LORD will guide you always; he will satisfy your needs in a
> sun-scorched land and will strengthen your frame. You will be like a
> well-watered garden, like a spring whose waters never fail. Your people

will rebuild the ancient ruins and will raise up the age-old foundations; you will be called Repairer of Broken Walls, Restorer of Streets with Dwellings (Isa. 58:8–12).

Recently I discussed this chapter with Dr R.T. Kendall, former senior minister of Westminster Chapel. I said, 'R.T., would it be accurate, would it be right for me to say that Isaiah 58 is an Old Testament picture of a sovereign revival?' 'Yes,' he said, 'unequivocally.'

So, can I challenge you? Many of you are reaching out into the community. Those of you who can, get involved; become a school governor, join a political party, stand for election as a local councillor. Stand as a Member of Parliament. This may not be appropriate for you, but you can pray that the Lord would raise up more labourers to go into that great field of harvest.

In Westminster, there are 1,200 gas lamps today – two 100-year-old lampstands – and there are three full-time engineers who travel around Westminster repairing these gas lamps. They are now electronically lit on a dark evening, but they're still there and they were the first gas lamps ever to be lit in Britain. The area of Westminster around the CARE offices and the Abbey and the Houses of Parliament, Dickens described as the Devil's Acre, a place of extraordinary filth, wickedness, debauchery, violence and crime. The Victorian government then started street lamps in Kensington. When I look at Westminster now, where the CARE offices are, just in the shadow of Big Ben, and the Abbey and Church House, it's one of the most salubrious areas of London. The pubs even close on a Saturday and Sunday! Once it was the Devil's Acre but it's been transformed, it's been turned around. If they can do that physically, we can do it spiritually. Areas of our national life are very dark. But in Christ's name we can let our light shine brightly, our good works, our social action, our gospel proclamation, this unique gospel of grace, and see our nation turn back to God.

The Addresses

Love your enemies

by David Coffey

David Coffey

David Coffey is the President of the Baptist World Alliance, and serves as an international pastor to believers in over 180 countries. Prior to this, he was General Secretary for the British Baptists for fifteen years. He first heard the call to Christian ministry at Keswick at the 1961 Convention, and proposed to his wife Janet at Keswick forty-four years ago, and he served on the Convention Council for ten years. His books include a commentary on Romans (IVP Crossway) and a new title in the Keswick Foundations series, called *All One in Christ Jesus*, a book calling for evangelical unity.

Love your enemies: Matthew 5:43–48

Introduction

When my grandchildren were younger I used to ask them, 'What is God's favourite number?' and they would say, 'Is it four, for the four Gospels? Is it twelve, for the twelve disciples? Is it sixty-six for the books of the Bible?' But the answer to the question, 'What is God's favourite number?' is number one. Because each one is special, each one is loved by God.

It's said that this passage, Matthew 5:43–48, is the very heart of the Sermon on the Mount. Of all the sayings, 'Love your enemies' was the one most quoted in the writings of the Early Church. 'Love your enemies' is known by people who never darken the door of a church. It comes to the very core of the Christian ethic; we're called to love people as God loves people without discrimination, because God's favourite number is number one. If you want to be like your heavenly Father, then you have to love people without discrimination.

An impossible command?

I want to say a pastoral word before we get into the meat of this passage. These powerful words 'Love your enemies' and 'Pray for those who persecute you' are a heavy burden for some. Some of you have been scarred and wounded by a toxic church war which has left a fellowship divided, and is still unreconciled. Some of you have experienced the trauma of domestic violence and brutal rape. Some of you, either personally or through loved ones, will have been caught up in the terrible street violence in some of our cities where young people, it seems, week after week, are stabbed to death.

Aled Jones on Radio 2 this morning reminded us of the memorial that was opened in Hyde Park last week, the 7 July 2005 memorial – the people who perished in the London tube and bus bombs. He talked about the Christian worker, Julie Nicholson, whose gifted musical daughter, Jenny, was one of the victims of that terrorist atrocity. She stepped down from Christian service; she didn't feel that she could face a Christian congregation with words of reconciliation and forgiveness when she said after the bombs, 'I felt very far from that.' She also described her anger: 'I rage that a human being could choose to take another human being's life. I rage that someone should do that in the name of God. I find that utterly offensive.'

If we move to the world scene, 'Love your enemies and pray for those who persecute you' . . . This year, in my international ministry, I've been to Egypt, Cuba, Chile and Romania, and in each of those places and many more, there are people who come to this passage with personal experience. They know that it's the most difficult and challenging thing. This is not an academic Bible study for them; it's a daily lived-out experience, loving the enemy, praying for the persecutor.

In India, some of the worst atrocities in the last two years against Christian believers have occurred in the state of Orissa. A pastor of twenty-five years who had refused to renounce his faith had a mob come to his home. They cut him into pieces, then they set his house on fire. His elderly mother, who was deaf and mute, was thrown on the fire when she tried to rescue him. So we need to come with pastoral sensitivity to these words of Jesus, 'Love your enemies and pray for those who persecute you'. Lord, are you giving us an impossible command for all those situations we've hinted at? Is there some way that you can lighten our burden? Come, we pray, into our hearts and into our thinking as we look at your word.

How do we love them? (vv. 43,44)

The word on the street

The first thing we see from Matthew 5:43 is this contrast between the word on the street and the word of Jesus. Jesus said, 'You have heard . . . it . . . said' – that's the word on the street. 'You've heard it said, love your neighbour and hate your enemy.' That is not a word from the Scriptures, it is found nowhere in the Old Testament. It was a phrase that had been invented by teachers of the Law to somehow ease the burden of the Law. The Old Testament said, 'Love your neighbour as yourself: I am the LORD' (Lev. 19:18), but the word on the street had become 'Love your neighbour and hate your enemy' and it was a very influential word. It became the common view, that you don't have to love all people. God's favourite number, number one, was forgotten by the people of God.

We know this phrase, 'You have heard it said.' We have words on the street not found in the Bible, and these words become very influential in our thinking; words like 'There can be no forgiveness for the enemy', 'Let them rot in hell', 'The enemy will never darken the door of my house' and 'As far as I'm concerned, the enemy is dead.' Soap operas thrive on this theme; soap operas are all nature and no grace. They thrive on ongoing hatred for the enemy who's destroyed fam-ily life. It's the word on the street. It's not the word of the Lord. And some of you know the powerful influence of this word on the street in the life of the church. It so shapes the thinking of people that they don't want to even raise the subject of the enemy: 'I don't even want to think about the enemy. I've drawn a line under the enemy. There can be no discussion regarding the enemy.' This is the contrast between the word on the street and the word of Jesus. Jesus says, 'You have heard . . . it . . . said . . . But I say to you, Love your enemies and pray for those who persecute you' (vv. 43,44).

The transforming initiative

If you follow the word of the street, nothing changes. The enemy remains the enemy. Whereas if you follow the word of Jesus,   you encounter what my friend Glen Stassen calls 'the transforming initiative'. All through his ministry, Jesus was engaged in the transforming initiative. The transforming initiative is Jesus seeing somebody with eyes of compassion, Jesus entering the world of that   person's bondage and then taking an initiative, which transforms the situation.

The demoniac

In Luke chapter 8, Jesus takes the transforming initiative with a hopeless case. This is the man who is demon possessed, he's naked, he cannot live inside a house, he lives inside the tombs. Jesus takes the transforming initiative to step into the cemetery and he fearlessly confronts the chained demoniac; he delivers the man, the enemy is cast out of this hopeless case, and Luke speaks of a community amazed at how they found him 'sitting at the feet of Jesus, clothed and in his right mind' (v. 35).

Zacchaeus

Jesus took a transforming initiative where there were deeply hated people, people like Zacchaeus.

Zacchaeus was hated in the community because he robbed people; he was the enemy in the community. As the chief tax collector, he had brought poverty and misery to many people. But Jesus meets him and greets him and eats with him; he visits his house and, at the end of a long day, announces to the crowd, 'salvation has come to this house' (Luke 19:9). It was a transforming initiative which put back into a poor community the wealth that had been taken from them. Zacchaeus says, 'Half of my possessions I give to the poor, and if I've robbed anyone then I'm going to repay you back four times more.' This is a transforming initiative which changed a life and transformed a community.

The woman at the well

What about the transforming initiative with despised outsiders? When Jesus met the woman at the well, John chapter 4, there were three things that made her a despised outsider: she was female, she was foreign, and she was flawed. She was female – and a strict rabbi wouldn't even greet his wife or daughter in public. She was foreign – Jews and Samaritans had no dealings with each other. She was flawed – she knew that her life was in a moral mess, but Jesus takes the transforming initiative with this despised outsider. He sees her with new eyes and steps into that world of moral bondage that she's in, and delivers her so that she's able to say that this person 'told me everything I ever did' (John 4:39). The community come to her and say, 'We no longer believe just because of what you said; now we have heard for ourselves, and we know that this man really is the Saviour of the world' (v. 42). Jesus' transforming initiative changing a life, transforming a community.

The very same principle of transforming initiative is at work in loving the enemy. It begins in Matthew 5:38. There was an old way of dealing with the enemy: the way of retribution. Legal retribution was an eye for an eye, a tooth for a tooth. But Jesus transforms that with this initiative: 'Don't resist an evil person.' If you're walking down the street and, in the custom of the day, somebody wants to shame you and slander you, and slaps you on the cheek, then turn the other cheek and offer that one. That's a transforming initiative. If you're taken to court unjustly and somebody wants to shame you and they take the coat off your back, not only give them the coat but – transforming initiative – give them your shirt as well. And as you stand there almost naked, you will not be the shamed one, they will be the shamed one. People will say, 'This has gone too far.' When you meet the Roman soldier, who by law was allowed to tap you on the shoulder and say, 'Carry my pack for a mile' – don't just carry it a mile, carry it a second mile. The transforming initiative will leave a Roman soldier, one of the hated enemies, totally amazed. These are transforming initiatives which change the situation.

Many years ago as a student, I was visiting the United States of America and, with another student, we were travelling and found ourselves in Memphis, Tennessee. There we were introduced through the church we were in to a man who had recently been converted; his name was Milton Thatcher, and he happened to be Elvis Presley's barber. I couldn't help but ask, 'Would you cut my hair?' I hoped it might improve my singing. He'd been a wrestler, and he'd turned up now as a barber.

One day, walking down the street, he came across some of his former drinking companions, and they said to him, 'Hey Milton, we hear that you've found religion.' And Milton said, 'I've become a Christian.'

One of them came up – remember he was in the wrestling world – and said, 'Is it true that the good book says that if I strike you on this cheek, you'll turn and offer me this cheek?' Milton said, 'That's true.' And the guy went on to say, 'If I strike you on this cheek, then you'll offer me this cheek?' and Milton said, 'That's true.' Then Milton got hold of his coat and said, 'But I'll tell you what, if ever I backslide, you're the first person I'm coming to look for.' I don't think that Milton had quite understood what Jesus was talking about. But let me remind you of the context of these words of Jesus, 'Love your enemies and pray for those who persecute you.'

It was a harsh time for the people listening to these words in that they were living in an occupied land. Rome ruled the country. Soldiers could be very violent; rapes and beatings were not uncommon, and so in this context of 'love the enemy', we're not only talking about Zacchaeus and people like him who robbed the poor, we're talking about people like soldiers who could menace the life of a family. Remember how Jesus appointed Simon the Zealot among the Twelve? Do you know what a Zealot was? The political philosophy of the Zealot was to drive the Romans into the sea. A true Zealot would have been prepared to take the life of his family if it advanced the cause of the party. So, to have Jesus saying, 'Love your enemies and pray for those who persecute you', it's as real as the situation some of you face. And Jesus now takes this transforming initiative: 'Love the enemy and pray for the person who's persecuting you.'

How does it begin?

There are many Greek words for that one English word, love: there's the word *storge* which is family love, there is the word *eros* which is sexual desire, there is the word *philea* which is the brotherly, sisterly love we feel for another person – so there is philanthropy and a common love for music, *philharmonia* – but Jesus doesn't choose to use any of those words, he chooses to use another word. All these words imply there's always something lovable or desirable in the object of love, but Jesus doesn't use this word. He uses the word *agape* which is the love without any reason. It's the love that is willed, it's the love that can only be born in the power of the Spirit. No matter how this person treats me, I will love this person. Whatever this person does, I will not stop loving them. You don't have to like a person to love them with *agape* love.

I wish you could meet my grandchildren. Rebecca, six years of age, was sitting at a meal not so long ago and turned to me and said, 'Granddad, you are doing more talking than eating' which I find utterly adorable. If *you* said it to me, I'd find it deeply offensive! But you see, there's something immensely lovable about this little child that's come into my life. We aren't talking about that kind of love; we're not in this world of family where love begins in the other person and their lovability draws out our love. *Agape* love begins in the heart. But how does it begin?

C.S. Lewis is helpful when he says we shouldn't spend time pondering whether we love our enemy, we should act as if we did. That's exactly what Jesus said: 'Love your enemies and pray for those who persecute you.' Jesus knew that love could only begin when we can begin to pray for the enemy. Prayer is the action that moves the will. Don't wait for love in your heart before you take a transforming initiative; it's your prayers that increase the love. In time, the power will be given to love the enemy too, to bless the persecutor, to forgive the enemy.

Because I was given this theme, it drew me back to that book and film that I haven't seen for years, *The Hiding Place*, which tells the story of Corrie ten Boom. It'll be known to you, this account which I'm going to use, you've heard it before, but listen to it in the context of this passage.

Corrie and her sister were prisoners in the concentration camp at Ravensbrück. There they suffered terrible atrocities. Corrie saw her sister Betsie die in the concentration camp. Corrie was eventually released around 1945 and felt God calling her to an evangelistic ministry, and one day she found herself in the German city of Munich. And in Corrie ten Boom's words, this is what happened.

> It was during the church service that I saw him. The former SS man who had stood guard at the shower room door in the processing centre at Ravensbrück. He was the first of our actual jailers that I had seen since I

left Ravensbrück. And suddenly it was all there, the room full of mocking men, the heaps of clothing, Betsie's pained, blanched face. He came up to me as the church was emptying, beaming and bowing. 'How grateful I am for your message, Fräulein,' he said, 'To think, as you say, he's washed my sins away.' His hand was thrust out to shake mine, and I, who had preached so often on the need to forgive, kept my hand at my side. Even as the angry vengeful thoughts boiled within me, I saw the sin of them. Christ had died for this man, and was I going to ask him for more? 'Lord Jesus,' I prayed, 'forgive me, and help me to forgive him.' I tried to smile. I struggled to raise my hand. I couldn't. I felt nothing, not the slightest spark of warmth or charity and so again I breathed a silent prayer, 'Jesus! I cannot forgive him. Grant me your forgiveness.' And as I took his hand, the most incredible thing happened. From my shoulder, along my arm and through my hand a current seemed to pass from me to him, while into my heart sprang a love for this stranger that almost overwhelmed me. And so I discovered that it's not on our forgiveness any more than on our goodness that the world's healing hinges, it's on his. When he tells us to love our enemies he gives, along with the command, he gives the love itself.[1]

Why should we love them? (vv. 45–47)

My dear brother and sister, I'm not expecting that one story will transform your situation, but I beg you to listen to what Jesus says in this passage as he explains why we are to love like this. Verse 45, we love the enemy because it's God-like. This is how we prove that we're children of our heavenly Father, we display the family likeness. God loves without discrimination. He sends his sun and his rain on evil people and on good people, on righteous and unrighteous people. When we love without discrimination we share God's character. God is generous even to the morally undeserving. His sun and rain are a sign of his common grace, and they're intended to draw people towards his saving grace in Jesus Christ. What a chaotic world it would be if God just sent his sun and rain on Christian farmers and their fields. The world's food supply and food chain would break down and we would have true chaos. That is the destructive power of discrimination, and this illustration comes from Jesus himself.

We are to be God-like because we are to remember our own story. Many of you have personal testimonies. You really were God's enemy and yet, whilst you were an enemy, he died for you. He washed you from your sins, he adopted you into his family, he commissioned you as ambassadors of the good news. Many believers, followers of Jesus, saved by grace, are living testimony that the enemy can be transformed into a friend and a family member in the family of God. But Jesus says more.

We love the enemy because we're called to a life of 'more than'. That's in verses 46 and 47; we belong to the 'more than' family. For Jesus is saying, 'What are you doing more than others?' He's referring to tax collectors and pagans who love their own friends and greet their own friends; in twentieth-century parlance, 'even cheats and swindlers have friends'. Cheats and swindlers enjoy loving relationships, good marriages, and they're generous with their money, and what Jesus is saying is, 'I want the "more than" in my disciples.' Loving your own kind and greeting your own friends, there's nothing exceptional in that. What is exceptional is loving the enemy, praying for those who persecute us, and the world is crying out for examples of that kind of discipleship.

A call to perfection (v. 48)

We live in a culture which cultivates retaliation, where hating the enemy is normal, and if we're going to be different – which is the call this week, to be radically different – we have to demonstrate that God does provide the power to love the enemy. And Jesus gives the third reason. We love the enemy because we're called to be perfect. These are the words of verse 48: 'be perfect, as your heavenly Father is   perfect.' It doesn't mean perfect in the sense of sinless perfection; I don't believe, according to the Sermon on the Mount, that we can have a perfect life without sin here on earth – no anger, no hatred, always loving the enemy . . . how can Jesus invite us in the early part of the sermon to go on hungering and thirsting for righteousness? It's because perfection, total life with God lies on the other side of glory, but meanwhile the call to be perfect

is a call to maturity, to completeness, to wholeness. It means a life totally at one with the will of God – a longing to fulfil the family likeness
and reflect it in our living; a desire to love without discrimination.

Looking to Jesus

Your question to me is, 'How can I leave Keswick this week with
some transforming initiative that I can take away with me, to go back
into that world where there are enemies?' And I say to you, 'Who is
saying these words? Whose words have we read, "Love your enemies
and pray for those who persecute you"?' Come and stand with me
under the cross at this moment, and look at Jesus who, when he was
mocked by his enemies didn't retaliate; who, when his enemies beat
him he took the pain; and, when his enemies nailed him to the cross,
he prayed for them. That was the transforming initiative of Jesus.

You know how familiar passages become to us – I hadn't spotted this
in Luke before. In Luke chapter 23:34, Jesus prayed, 'Father, forgive
them, for they know not what they do' and in verse 48, after Jesus died,
the people on Golgotha 'beat their breasts and went away'. Ask yourself
this question: Would they have done this if Jesus had not prayed for
them? Was it not the prayer for the enemy that distressed them? He
could have cursed them. He could have threatened them. He could have
called down God's judgement on them. But he prayed for his enemies.
We're saying to each other, 'Lord, how can we get to the place where we
can pray for the enemy?' I suggest we hold the broken pieces in our
hands before the Lord as a sign, and pray that in his time and in his way,
he would reveal to our hearts a transforming initiative that would bring
healing to our own lives and transform the situations that so burden us.

Notes

[14] Corrie Ten Boom, *TheHiding Place* (London: Hodder & Stoughton, 1975).

No one can serve two masters

by Conrad Mbewe

Conrad Mbewe

Conrad Mbewe trained as a mining engineer. In 1987, he started to pastor the Kabwata Baptist Church, and has worked there for the last twenty-one years, seeing the church grow from thirty-five members to well over three hundred. Apart from this pastorate, Conrad exercises a global itinerant preaching ministry. He has contributed chapters to various books, is the editor of the *Reformation Zambia* magazine, and writes three columns in two weekly national newspapers in Zambia. He is also the Principal of the Reformed Baptist Preachers college. Conrad is married to Felistas, and they have three teenage children.

No one can serve two masters: Matthew 6:19–24

Introduction

In Matthew chapter 6, the Lord Jesus Christ issues a clear warning to all his disciples: there is a serious danger which threatens our walk with him. This danger arises because of the material things which surround us – that we might love these things, and in the process be robbed of our love for the Lord our God.

The Lord is not really saying that there's something sinful in wealth, in temporal materials; it is the inordinate affection that we may have towards these things that the Lord is clearly warning against. The apostle Paul, in 1 Timothy chapter 6 speaks about the love of the things of this world: '. . . the love of money is a root of all kinds of evil' (v. 10). It is this which the Lord is seeking to warn us against because it is the blight of the soul; it destroys us from the inside out.

True spirituality

It is a confirmed fact that where Christians have suffered persecution or lack of basic necessities, often, a few years later, you find an enriched form of spirituality. But where God has blessed his people materially, instead of finding a people that are full of God and full of thanksgiving to him, instead you find warped souls, souls that have been drained of spirituality; people taken up with the toys of the world at the expense of their own souls. Why is that so? The Lord Jesus, in Matthew chapter 6, gives us the answer.

We're looking through the great Sermon on the Mount. Having dealt with the Beatitudes, the description of a Christian, having shown us the duty that arises from that, that we are both salt and light, the Lord Jesus gives some basic standards to true spirituality: 'For I tell you that unless your righteousness surpasses that of the Pharisees and the teachers of the law, you will certainly not enter the kingdom of heaven' (Matt. 5:20).

Three thieves

It is after that that the Lord Jesus spends some time dealing with the thieves of eternal rewards. He gives us three thieves that are likely, while we are continuing as his people, to rob us of an abundant entrance into God's kingdom.

The first is ostentation, which he deals with in terms of our giving to people, our praying and our fasting (6:1–18). The second is essentially materialism – worldliness; a love for things that are temporal and physical in this world (vv. 19–24). And the third, which in many ways is the opposite of the second, is worry, anxiety – 'What shall we eat? What shall we drink? What shall we wear? What is it that will sustain us tomorrow?' (vv. 25–34) – a sense of insecurity that robs us of energy for today because we are worried about tomorrow.

It is the second that we are dealing with here – that the things that God blesses us with can easily become a snare to us; that instead of blessing us, they can become a curse. Therefore, we need to beware.

Wrong investments

Why should the physical temporal blessings of God end up being a source of the dryness of our own souls? The Lord gives us the answers and they're very plain in this passage. First of all, it is because materialism kills true spirituality by fixing our hearts on a place where investment may be temporarily, and certainly eternally, lost. That's why Jesus urges his disciples to invest in heaven: 'Do not store up for yourselves treasures on earth, where moth and rust destroy, and where thieves break in and steal' (v. 19). He's appealing here to basic common sense.

A lack of wisdom

One of the experiences that our own African political leaders have had for well over two decades has been a failure to harness the potential of investors outside of the African continent. And the reason is simple: it's because western businessmen consider investing in Africa too risky; they would rather hang on to the money. 'Africa is unpredictable,' they say. 'One moment all may be well, in the next moment there is civil war.'

Jesus is basically saying, 'Look at the people of the world, look at the way in which they are very careful with respect to where they place their investment. You, as my children, ought to be wiser than them.' Jesus is telling us here that pouring our lives into things that are merely for this life, where moth and rust destroy and thieves break in and steal, speaks of a lack of wisdom.

James chapter 5 gives us a similar warning: 'Now listen, you rich people, weep and wail because of the misery that is coming upon you. Your wealth has rotted, and moths have eaten your clothes. Your gold and silver are corroded. Their corrosion will testify against you and eat your flesh like fire. You have hoarded wealth in the last days. Look! The wages you failed to pay the workmen who mowed your fields are crying out against you. The cries of the harvesters have reached the ears of the Lord Almighty. You have lived on earth in luxury and self-indulgence. You have fattened yourselves in the day of slaughter. You have condemned and murdered innocent men, who were not opposing you' (Jas. 5:1–6).

Even apart from the injustice, there is the clear statement here of gold and silver corroding and, ultimately, the hoarded wealth being useless because it has been eaten away. Some individuals have poured their entire wealth into one form of investment or another, only to wake up one day and find that the economic machine has turned in the opposite direction and, consequently, all that they have hoarded has been swept away.

But that's not all there is in respect to moth and rust and thieves.

A matter of time

This life is temporal. However much God may bless us with a long life, it is but a probation period; it will soon be over. Death soon takes us away from everything that we've ever gathered in this life. Human thieves may rob us of things, but they always leave us with *something*. But when death comes to take us from our treasure, we experience something of what Job said when he said, 'Naked I came from my mother's womb, and naked I shall depart' (Job 1:21).

Where then is wisdom in the life of an individual who pours his everything merely into this temporal existence, knowing very well that sooner rather than later, 'I must go from this life into the next'? Surely wisdom dictates that we should think about the life hereafter, that which is permanent? That's what the Lord Jesus Christ advises his people in Matthew 6:20 when he says, 'But store up for yourselves treasures in heaven, where moth and rust do not destroy, and where thieves do not break in and steal.' The glory of heaven lies in that it is an eternal, blissful existence, one that will never, ever end. And he who invests in that place will not only find his investment there but finds it multiplied thirty-fold, sixty-fold, indeed a hundred-fold.

Therefore, if you are truly a child of God and you know that you are going to heaven, it only makes sense that you should ask the question, 'How can I take worldly wealth and so use it, so invest it, that when this life is over, I will find it kept in heaven for me, having been multiplied by the hands of the living God?' I trust you have an answer to that question. I trust that you have already taken seriously the words of the Lord Jesus Christ because, as he goes on to tell us here, 'where your treasure is, there your heart will be also' (v. 21). In other words, if you invest in heaven, your heart, your devotion, is tied up with that place of permanence, that place of bliss, that place of reward, that place of true eternal prosperity. On the other hand, if out of love for this world you have poured everything into that which is temporal, when death comes to smudge you from this life, oh what pain, oh what loss, oh what misery will be yours! Nothing to show, as you go from this life into the next, for the twenty, thirty, forty, sixty, eighty, perhaps even 100 years that God may have given you on earth. Surely, that speaks about a lack of wisdom.

That's the first thing that our Saviour draws our attention to: materialism fails us in that it makes us invest in a place where we will experience loss. It's just a matter of time.

Worldliness

Secondly, materialism kills true spirituality because it blinds us to eternal reality and, consequently, takes us on a downward spiral of worldliness. The Lord Jesus Christ puts it this way in 6:22,23: 'The eye is the lamp of the body. If your eyes are good, your whole body will be full of light. But if your eyes are bad, your whole body will be full of darkness. If then the light within you is darkness, how great is that darkness!'

Blurred vision

What is Jesus talking about here? It's the fact that you need good eyes in order to be attracted to and mesmerised by beauty, loveliness, splendour and magnificence. Bad eyes rob you of the capacity to look at a beautiful thing and go, 'Wow!' You can't see, your vision is blurred; others are drinking in the beauty before them and consequently responding appropriately to it, but you are passing by in complete dullness. This is precisely what materialism does; it blurs your vision so that you are blinded to spiritual profundities and immensities. It dulls your spiritual perception; it removes the edge from your spiritual appetite and, as a result, you end up trusting in money, which is completely unreliable, instead of trusting in God, who is eternally faithful.

The apostle Paul urged Timothy to warn those who were rich, to ensure that they did not allow their wealth to have this effect upon them

> Command those who are rich in this present world not to be arrogant
> nor to put their hope in wealth, which is so uncertain, but to put their
> hope in God, who richly provides us with everything for our enjoy-
> ment. Command them to do good, to be rich in good deeds, and to
> be generous and willing to share. In this way they will lay up treasure
> for themselves as a firm foundation for the coming age, so that they
> may take hold of the life that is truly life (1 Tim. 6:17–19).

Jesus is basically saying that the way in which you are functioning right
now speaks about your spiritual perception. If you are truly weaned
away from the world, though you are in it, faith is able to give you sight
of things eternal, things spiritual, that will enable you to so relate to the
world around you that you will want to invest in the things that really
matter. But when you are carried away with the temporal things of this
world, you lose sight of that perception; you start to value people by
their bank balances rather than by the fact that they are made in God's
image. If you are in that state and still believing all is well with you, you
will finally get a rude awakening – when it is too late.

Remember the rich fool that Jesus spoke about – an individual
who God blessed so abundantly that he had a better harvest than he
had ever anticipated? As he looked at the problem of where to store
this abundance, he decided, 'Well, I'm destroying my small barn and
putting up something much bigger, putting all my harvest in there and
then saying to myself, "Take life easy; eat, drink and be merry."' He
was seeing himself simply sitting back, having a holiday that lasted 365
days a year, 24/7. But God said to him, 'You fool! Tonight, you're coming into eternity and who is going to benefit from all this?' Jesus says,
'That's the way it's going to be with everyone who is rich in terms of
this world's wealth but not rich towards God.'

Oh, may God not say to any one of us, 'You fool!' We've had sufficient warning from his word preached. We've had sufficient warning
from the reading of the Scriptures. There's no reason why we should
continue in this life insisting that everything is all right with us when,
in actual fact, our spiritual eyes are dim and it is the things of this
world that determine our lives.

Spiritual eyes

Thankfully, although verses 22 and 23 are largely negative, Jesus also gives us a positive statement. He says, 'If your eyes are good, your whole body will be full of light.' We shouldn't miss that because the point is that when faith is in the best shape, in the midst of all the noise of this world – the multiplicity of toys that the world is constantly throwing at us – God enables us to see through it all for its froth and mist and dew. He enables us to still see that solid joys and lasting treasure are only found by those who have their eyes fixed on Jesus. And consequently we walk through life lightly; we walk through life appreciating that even those who are materially poor, if they are in Jesus, are spiritually rich because they have the unsearchable riches of Christ. And similarly, like Moses of old, we will prefer to suffer present loss for the sake of Christ rather than own the treasures of Egypt, simply because faith enables us to look beyond time and see the reward that awaits us in eternity. Like Christians across the ages, we will gladly suffer imprisonment, gladly suffer the confiscation of our property – for the sake of Christ.

Once, David Livingstone, who brought Christianity to my part of the world, was on a brief break from the mission field, back in the UK, speaking about the need for missionaries. And somebody asked him what he had sacrificed for the sake of the kingdom. Livingstone's answer was, 'Sacrifice? Sacrifice? You and I dare not speak about sacrifice in the light of the sacrifice of God's own Son.' In other words, his eyes looked beyond the temporal, looked beyond that which was around him when he was in the jungles of Africa, looked beyond the fact that, even at that moment, his arm was in a sling because a lion had sought to maul him to death. And he saw him who is invisible, the reward that lay ahead of him; saw him who sits at the right hand of the majesty on high, looking like a lamb that was slain. With eyes – spiritual eyes – like that, Livingstone willingly got on the ship once again, heading out to the very place where he had survived the attack of a lion. That's what will be true of you when your spiritual eyes are full of light and, consequently, your whole being is able to see life from a spiritual perspective.

Love destroyer

Another reason that materialism kills true spirituality is because it strikes at the root of all true religion by destroying our love for God. This is what Jesus meant by the wake-up call in verse 24, when he said we cannot love two masters: 'No one can serve two masters. Either he will hate the one and love the other, or he will be devoted to the one and despise the other. You cannot serve both God and Money.'

Inch by inch

Materialism kills spirituality by inches. Do you know the story of the Arab's camel? In the middle of the night, because of the cold, it put its head into its master's tent. The tent was rather small and the master, feeling sorry for his camel, moved a little bit to give it room. And while he was enjoying his sleep, the camel was still making its way in. Consequently, the Arab moved a little bit more. Well, soon the whole camel was inside the tent, and the Arab was outside. Once you allow the world a place in your affections, inch by inch, you will discover yourself despising and hating what you will be calling 'the strictness of Christianity'. You will want a Christian faith that walks around in silver slippers, one that is to your convenience. Anything that begins to suggest sacrifice, holiness and godliness, despising the world, you will begin to look down on as 'fanaticism'. The truth is, the world has taken your heart away from God.

In Luke chapter 18, Jesus, speaking to the rich young ruler, said to him, 'You still lack one thing. Sell everything you have and give to the poor, and you will have treasure in heaven. Then come, follow me' (v. 22). The Bible tells us that, when he heard this, he became very sad because he was a man of great wealth. He was an individual who, when he was asked the question, 'Do you obey the commandments – do not commit adultery, do not murder, do not steal?' replied, 'All these I have kept since I was a boy' (v. 21) but the Lord knew that his heart was in the wrong place and, when he put a finger on his wealth, the man abandoned the Lord and went off with that which is temporal.

This is what made Judas betray the Master – thirty pieces of silver; this is what made Demas abandon the apostle Paul – he loved the present world (2 Tim. 4:10). Don't cheat yourself! Don't think that you can keep these two together – you can't. 'Yes,' that's what the devil will say to you; 'Yes,' that's what the world will say to you. Don't believe it. James uses very strong language when he says, 'You adulterous people, don't you know that friendship with the world is hatred toward God? Anyone who chooses to be a friend of the world becomes an enemy of God. Or do you think Scripture says without reason that the spirit he caused to live in us envies intensely?' (Jas. 4:4,5) Or, as the apostle John puts it, in his first epistle: 'Do not love the world or anything in the world. If anyone loves the world, the love of the Father is not in him. For everything in the world – the cravings of sinful man, the lust of his eyes and the boasting of what he has and does – comes not from the Father but from the world. The world and its desires pass away, but the man who does the will of God lives forever' (1 John 2:15–17). You cannot love God and love the world at the same time. Don't try to do the impossible. No one before you has succeeded, no one after you will succeed – neither will you.

All our hearts

This is Christ's call to all of us, with respect to radical discipleship: he wants us to give him all our hearts, and isn't that what the greatest commandment really is? 'Love the Lord your God with all your heart and with all your soul and with all your strength and with all your mind' (Luke 10:27). That's the call that God gives to each one of us – to give him our all – and consequently his message here is clear: deal drastically, deal today, with any inordinate affection in your soul for this world's riches, before it deals a death blow to your love for God and leaves you an eternal pauper. If the world, like that camel, has slowly been entering into your life, suffocating any spiritual reality within you, dulling your senses, reducing you to a Christianity of convenience, press the alarm today!

The cure

All of us must be asking the question 'What is the best cure?' because the world is all around us, with all the noise seeking to draw our hearts and minds away from God, to fill our lives with things that are temporal. And here is our Master saying, 'Don't store up your riches on earth. Have spiritual eyes that are alive and in the best shape to keep yourself going.' Beware of the lie of loving the world and loving God at the same time. You may ask, 'But how can I keep away from going in that direction?' The answer's clear: 'By keeping your eyes on Calvary, looking at the love wherewith God has loved us.'

Meditate much on the cross; think again concerning the price that God himself has paid out of love for your soul: 'For God so loved the world that he gave his one and only Son, that whoever believes in him shall not perish but have eternal life' (John 3:16). That God should sacrifice the best of heaven for the worst of earth, that he should not consider his own Son but give him up for us all . . . how can we want to hold back our love? How can we want to give our love, our affections, to temporal things, things that will perish with time, in the light of the fact that an eternal God has given of his very self for us? Surely love must respond to love.

Has the cross melted your heart? Has the cross drawn you from the froth and mist and dew of this world, and made you sense that God - Father, Son and Holy Spirit – alone is worth living for, alone is worth dying for, if it means a thousand deaths? Have you gazed sufficiently at that cross to then turn around and look at this world, and everything around dims into insignificance? *There* is the cure: the Christianity of the cross; the cross of the Christian faith.

And therefore, like Elijah of old, I challenge you today to give your entire mind and heart and body to this Saviour, who hung upon the cross for you. He alone has loved you with an everlasting love. Therefore get rid of your idols; they've done nothing for your soul. Instead, love him back. Gaze afresh at the cross, until you view the mercy of God with all its abundance; until you sense something of the flood of God's love pouring upon your soul again.

May God win us all from the froth of this world and produce from among us preachers, missionaries, martyrs, and a Christian faith that is unstoppable because we have beheld him who is invisible!

The trials of life

by Paul Williams

Paul Williams

Paul Williams worked in the newspaper industry before studying at Oak Hill Theological College in London. After several years at Christ Church Ware, and St Peter's, Harold Wood, he served at All Souls, Langham Place in London. Paul is now Vicar of Christ Church Fulwood in Sheffield. He is co-author of the book *If You Could Ask God One Question*. Paul is married to Caroline and they have three children. Paul is a keen tennis player and supports Leeds United football club.

The trials of life: Genesis 39 – 40

Introduction

'It came as quite a shock as a new Christian to discover that living a faithful Christian life made life a lot harder sometimes.' These are the words of someone who explained how doing the right thing at work resulted in the company telling him that his services would no longer be needed. That experience left him wondering if God was really with him, if God was really in control, if God really loved him. It's going to happen, sooner or later, to all of us who seek to live a Christian life – doing the right thing will make life harder, not easier, for us.

It's not difficult to imagine the scenario; you're a student, in this difficult tough economic climate, looking for a job. You've finally got an interview. It looks like the perfect job, the interview's going very well, and then the interviewer asks you about where it mentions in your CV that you were a part of the Christian Union at university, and how you attend your local church. The interviewer says, 'Don't tell me you're one of those born-again Christians!' and when you say you are, the whole tone of the interview changes. Needless to say, you don't get offered the job.

For those who are in the workplace, maybe you're asked to do something you think is ethically dubious. Politely but firmly you refuse to do it and, from that moment on, you are overlooked for promotion. Or, as is happening all over the Muslim world right now, you say you're a Christian and your family disown you, you're ostracized by society – or worse.

Earlier this year I heard Archbishop Ben Kwashi speaking. He's the archbishop of northern Nigeria. He was explaining what it means to be a Christian in his part of the world. He said, 'On the way to church you have stones thrown at you. When you arrive at church, the first thing you have to do is to clean away the human excrement that has been deliberately smeared on all the seats.' If we live a faithful Christian life, one way or another, we are going to get a hard time for it.

The normal Christian life

Suffering as a result of righteous living is the normal Christian life, and God is with us. That is the big thrust of Genesis chapters 39 and 40. Now, in chapter 39, things are not going well for Joseph. Humanly speaking, his life is a disaster, a far cry from the life he enjoyed at the beginning of chapter 37. Back then, he was so cocksure of himself; the favourite son of his father. God had spoken to him through dreams and had told him, against all the cultural norms of the day, that his whole family would bow down to him and serve him. He'd blurted out his dreams to his brothers and to his dad and, from that moment on, things had gone pear-shaped, with his brothers selling him to Midianite merchants who, in turn, sold him into slavery in Egypt. 'Now Joseph had been taken down to Egypt. Potiphar, an Egyptian who was one of Pharaoh's officials, the captain of the guard, bought him from the Ishmaelites who had taken him there' (39:1).

Joseph, then, is a slave in Potiphar's household and chapters 39 and 40 are a series of events that leave Joseph at rock bottom. Just when you think he's fallen about as far as anyone can fall, he falls further. From slavery to Potiphar, he ends up in prison (39:20). And, by the end of chapter 40, even though he has interpreted the dream of the chief cupbearer to the king, we read, 'The chief cupbearer, however, did not remember Joseph; he forgot him' (40:23).

A model believer

Things seem desperate for Joseph: a slave, a prisoner, a forgotten man. His life is a disaster. But here's the big thing about these two chapters. In chapters 39 and 40, Joseph has been a model believer; he doesn't deserve any of this to have happened to him. The reason he is in this state is – wait for it – because he has been faithful to God. In chapter 37, you could argue that he deserved what he got; frankly, he was a spoiled brat. But not here. These chapters are about a man who has done nothing wrong, who has remained faithful to God, yet nothing has gone right for him.

Now look how that pans out. Joseph works so hard and so honestly in Potiphar's house that we read that Potiphar 'left in Joseph's care everything he had; with Joseph in charge, he did not concern himself with anything except the food he ate' (39:6). Joseph is an exemplary slave. Potiphar came to trust him.

When tempted by Potiphar's wife to have sex with her, look how he answers: 'No-one is greater in this house than I am. My master has withheld nothing from me except you, because you are his wife. How then could I do such a wicked thing and sin against God?' (39:9) Joseph refuses to cheat on his master. Even as Potiphar's wife throws herself at him, he is the model believer. Yet it is his refusal to sleep with Potiphar's wife that leads him to be thrown into jail. He does the right thing and it ends in him being a foreigner in an alien jail, banged up in prison with a criminal record and with no right of appeal.

And then in jail, when you might expect him to moan and groan about the injustice of it all, he lives a life that is so impressive that the prison warder 'paid no attention to anything under Joseph's care, because the LORD was with Joseph and gave him success in whatever he did' (39:23).

In these chapters, Joseph lives a remarkably impressive life. Even in prison he takes his responsibilities, his opportunities, to witness to God. When two prisoners have dreams and want someone to interpret them, Joseph's first words to them are: 'Do not interpretations belong to God?' (40:8)

The Lord was with Joseph

Joseph is a model believer but, as we've seen in chapter 40 verse 23, it all ends in him imprisoned and forgotten. He might well have believed that God had abandoned him. But look what we are told in chapter 39: 'The LORD was with Joseph' (v. 2); 'his master saw that the LORD was with him' (v. 3); 'Joseph's master took him and put him in prison, the place where the king's prisoners were confined. But while Joseph was there in the prison, the LORD was with him' (vv. 20,21); 'The warder paid no attention to anything under Joseph's care, because the LORD was with Joseph' (v. 23).

You can't miss it, can you? 'The Lord was with Joseph.' It is a constant refrain and we get the same message in chapter 40. Joseph rightly says to Pharaoh's chief cupbearer and to his baker that God alone gives interpretation to dreams (40:8) and then we see that Joseph is able to interpret the dreams. So it is obvious that God is with Joseph, or he wouldn't have been able to interpret the dreams.

Suffering: the way of Christ

Everything in the Bible tells us that God is with Joseph, but everything in the circumstances tempts is to believe that God has abandoned him because, when Joseph does what is right, everything goes wrong. And here we have a paradigm, a pattern, for the Christian life: righteous living, living right before God, will result in suffering, and when suffering comes it does not mean that God has abandoned us. We know that, because hundreds of years later, we saw the supreme example of this in Jesus.

Listen to how Isaiah prophesied in chapter 53: 'He was despised and rejected by men, a man of sorrows, and familiar with suffering . . . we considered him stricken by God, smitten by him, and afflicted' (vv. 3,4). But what does Isaiah say a few verses later? 'Yet it was the LORD's will to crush him and cause him to suffer, and though the LORD makes his life a guilt offering, he will see his offspring and prolong his days, and the will of the LORD will prosper his hand' (v. 10). It happened to Jesus.

In 1 Peter 2:22,23, we see how the New Testament makes this very point, that it is the normal Christian life to suffer. Again, speaking of Jesus: 'He committed no sin, and no deceit was found in his mouth. When they hurled their insults at him, he did not retaliate; when he suffered, he made no threats. Instead, he entrusted himself to him who judges justly.'

Innocent suffering was the way of Christ. Had God abandoned Jesus? Of course not! This is the way of God's salvation and it is the pattern for all believers, and that's actually Peter's point here. Look back to verse 19

> '. . . it is commendable if a man bears up under the pain of unjust suffering because he is conscious of God. But how is it to your credit if you receive a beating for doing wrong and endure it? But if you suffer for doing good and you endure it, this is commendable before God. To this you were called, because Christ suffered for you, leaving you an example, that you should follow in his steps' (1 Pet. 2:19–21).

'To this you were called' – do you hear it? To follow in the footsteps of the Lord Jesus Christ is to suffer unjustly, to suffer for when you live a righteous life.

Abandoned?

When that happens – and it *will* happen, if we do live a righteous life – we will invariably be tempted to believe that God has somehow abandoned us. Look how Peter writes to this group of persecuted Christians who are suffering just because they are believers. In 1 Peter 4:12 he says, 'Dear friends, do not be surprised at the painful trial you are suffering, as though something strange were happening to you.' Don't be surprised when you suffer for being a Christian. The surprise is not when Christians suffer for being Christian; the surprise is when Christians don't suffer at all. Suffering for doing the right thing is the pattern of the Christian life. Verses 13,14: 'But rejoice that you participate in the sufferings of Christ, so that you may be overjoyed when his glory is revealed. If you are insulted because of the name of Christ, you are blessed, for the Spirit of glory and of God rests on you.' When I suffer, does it mean that

God has left me? No, the Spirit of God is on me. That's what it means when I'm suffering because I'm living a righteous life.

Just think what a difference it would make if we really believed that. People regularly come to me, when they are suffering, and say, 'Does it mean that God has left me?' When things are tough, people often conclude that God has abandoned them or that he isn't in control or that he doesn't love them. That is not the truth.

It's not helped by some teaching that has become very popular in some highly successful churches in Britain today. Their great refrain is this: 'God wants to bless you.' Of course he wants to bless you. But listen to what they mean by that: 'If you are out of a job, he wants to give you a job; if you don't have much money, pray for it, he'll give you money; if you don't have good health, you pray and he'll give you good health. He wants to make everything go well for you.' It's the old-fashioned prosperity gospel. It's not true.

To this you were called, that you would suffer, following the footsteps of Christ. Right through the Bible, we see the pattern of the Christian life is that we will suffer for righteous living and, when we do, God is with us. Are you suffering, just because you're a Christian? God is with you, he hasn't abandoned you. Suffering as a result of righteous living is the normal Christian life, and God is with us.

Overcoming sin and living for God

Suffering as a result of righteous living helps us overcome sin, and then to live for God's will. 'Therefore, since Christ suffered in his body, arm yourselves also with the same attitude, because he who has suffered in his body is done with sin. As a result, he does not live the rest of his earthly life for evil human desires, but rather for the will of God' (1 Pet. 4:1,2).

Do you see what Peter is saying here? 'Christ suffered physically for doing good; we should be ready for that, too. Then, when we do suffer physically for doing good, we will overcome sin.' That's what we will see in Joseph in a moment. The point is really very simple: once you've suffered for the Lord, you are more ready to live the whole of your life, the rest of your life, uncompromised by sin.

A man I know, as a new Christian, was told by his boss to sack someone who really shouldn't have been sacked. In the past, he'd done it without questioning but now he was a Christian, he wouldn't do it. It was a really big step for him, to stand up to his boss and do the right thing. That was a tough thing to do; it seriously affected his career prospects. But now, some years later, ask him about it and he'll tell you that he was pleased he did it. He'll tell you that, having done the right thing once, it was easier to do the right thing the next time. Because now, he does not live life for human desires (see 1 Pet. 4:2). He is no longer driven by the need for the approval of his boss, no longer has this desperate desire for promotion; that doesn't have a hold over him any more. Because he made a costly decision, it is easier now to live for Christ.

Every time you make a decision not to sin, it will be easier not to sin the next time. It takes time to form Christian character. Now, we see that happening in Joseph. There are three temptations here: the temptations of power, sex and despair. As we look at these temptations, remember this: as we overcome sin, it will help us to live for God, to stand against sin, in the future.

Power

Because sex is the one that dominates here, it's very easy to miss this one, but this is a very big and significant temptation. Joseph was a slave in Potiphar's house. Twice we're told that Potiphar was the captain of the guard (37:36; 39:1). Potiphar was the commander-in-chief, if you like, one of the most powerful men in the most powerful nation on the face of the earth.

So Joseph had come to the centre of power and, as the story unfolds, we see there are two examples of how power is used. There's a bad example and there's a good example. The bad example is Potiphar's wife: '. . . after a while, his master's wife took notice of Joseph and said, "Come to bed with me!" ' (39:7). It isn't an invitation, it is a command. There are actually just two words in the original. What she actually says is something like this: 'Sex now!' It's about power; it's about Potiphar's wife using her power. In her world, she is very powerful, she always gets what she wants, and she wants Joseph now.

Having power and influence over others is a very dangerous thing, and Potiphar's wife misuses power. But now look at Joseph. He is a great example of the use of power. And the reason this is so significant is, as we see the story unfolding, Joseph is going to have huge power. Can he be trusted with it? If he overcomes the temptation to sin in the area of power now, he will be able to be trusted with power in the future. Look at Joseph's power: 'Potiphar put him in charge of his household, and he entrusted to his care everything he owned' (39:4). Joseph, then, has power over the household of one of the most powerful men in the whole world. But look how Joseph uses his power (v. 5); 'From the time he put him in charge of his household and of all that he owned, the LORD blessed the household of the Egyptian because of Joseph.' That's how to use power, in order to bless others. The word 'blessing' here makes us think of the great blessing to Abraham, Genesis chapter 12: the three-fold blessing, that from Abraham, his descendants would become a great nation, numerically great, that they would come into the Promised Land and that, through one of his descendants, all nations would be blessed. Here is a glimpse of God fulfilling that promise. We know it's going to happen supremely through Jesus, but here is just a glimpse of one of Abraham's descendants, Joseph, blessing the nations and, crucially in these moments, Joseph proves that he will not misuse power.

How are you using *your* power? Are you using it to bless? Are you using it in line with the promises to Abraham, where God promised to bring a numerically great people into the Promised Land, into eternity in the new creation, to enjoy the blessing of knowing God through Jesus Christ? That's what you've been given power for. Yet, strangely, I hear some Christians telling me that they can't invite those under them at work to Christian events because that would be an abuse of their authority. No, that would be exactly the right use of the authority God has given. Use power to bless others, even if it results in you suffering yourself. There is no greater blessing you can give somebody than to invite them to the Lord Jesus.

Sex

You don't need me to tell you that this is a huge temptation in society today. And it is a huge temptation that perpetually sees Christians fall. When I was working in London, at All Souls, Langham Place, I had Christians walk into my study and confess every possible sexual sin except bestiality (sex with an animal). Fornication, sex before marriage, I heard that many times. Adultery, I heard that too many times as well. Paedophilia, I heard that once or twice. Homosexual sin, I counselled a number of men who were suffering with that. And one man walked in and told me he'd been sleeping with a prostitute. These men had a testimony of how they became Christians. These men were involved in Bible study. They were fully involved in the life of the church.

You probably won't be surprised to hear me say that the most prolific problem of the lot, in the sexual arena, is internet pornography. I've spoken with so many Christian men who're struggling with this. Tim Chester ran a seminar on dealing with pornography and here, in the Convention handbook, is a quote: 'One survey suggests 50 per cent of Christian men have used pornography.' I'm not surprised by that statistic because I meet so many Christian men who tell me. I reckon for every Christian man that tells me about that, there must be another big bunch, who've never told me because it's a hard thing to tell the pastor. Sexual sin is a huge problem in our churches.

Joseph was tempted in this very area but he overcame. Remember who Joseph was – he was 'well-built and handsome' (39:6), he had a six-pack, rippling muscles, a beautifully bronzed body and he was good-looking. In chapter 37, we read that he was 17 years old (37:2). So by chapter 39, here's a handsome, well-built man in his late teenage years or early twenties. This temptation came to Joseph at the time when he was a hot-blooded bag of testosterone, at the height of his sexual prime, and yet he stood firm. Isn't that impressive? How did he do it?

Notice the nature of sexual temptation. It is unpredictable, it can come to us quite out of the blue. Verse 7: 'Joseph was well-built and handsome, and after a while his master's wife took notice of Joseph and said, "Come to bed with me!"' This sexual temptation came from nowhere. You're surfing the net, quite legitimately, and out of nowhere there's a link to a really most unhelpful and quite in-your-face sort of website, screaming at you, 'Sex now!' Sexual temptation is unpredictable.

Secondly, it's persistent. Verse 10: '. . . she spoke to Joseph day after day'. It's not difficult to imagine Potiphar's wife, one day, in an unnecessarily low-cut dress, leaning over Joseph while he was at his desk doing the accounts, whispering in his ear; another day, coming out of the bathroom in a bathrobe, asking Joseph to help her with the shower curtain and making suggestive remarks as they go their way; another day, stepping out of the pool in her swimsuit, putting her arm around Joseph and telling him she feels hot . . . And it happened day after day. Sexual temptation is persistent. You can say no and it can come back again, and it will wear you down.

Thirdly, we see that sexual temptation is opportunistic: 'One day he went into the house to attend to his duties, and none of the household servants was inside. She caught him by his cloak and said, "Come to bed with me!"' (vv. 11,12) Do you see how she takes advantage of the situation, when no one else is around?

You're working late at night at the office, there's no one else there. You're away on a business trip, you feel lonely in the hotel. You're having a rough time in your marriage and suddenly there's someone who's showing interest in you. That is the nature of sexual temptation: unpredictable, persistent, opportunistic.

The way to overcome sexual temptation is to learn from Joseph – he calls sin 'sin'. Verse 9: 'No-one is greater in this house than I am. My master has withheld nothing from me except you, because you are his wife. How then could I do such a wicked thing and sin against God?' Joseph calls a spade a spade; he calls sin 'sin', great wickedness. Watch the danger when you start to call it something else; when you tell yourself that it will relieve some tension; when you persuade yourself that these pictures are on the internet anyway and it won't do anybody any harm; when you begin to tell yourself that it's love.

I think of a minister who fell sexually with someone in his church. After the sorry affair, he spent time with a friend, helping him through the mess that he'd made of his life. His friend told him how wicked it was and he said, 'I've always believed that, but it's so hard to believe it was wrong because it felt so good.' We must call sin 'sin', we must call it what it is, we must call it wicked.

The second way he overcame sexual temptation – he remained faithful to his master. Joseph remained faithful to his earthly master and, most importantly, to his heavenly Master. You'll see it there in verse 9: 'I can't do this to my master.' He knew the hurt it would cause.

When the minister I just mentioned said, 'It's hard to believe it was wrong because it felt so good', his friend said this to him: 'Look at the pain you've caused to your wife and to this woman's husband. Think of the agony you've brought upon your children and her children. Consider the way your actions have left the church distraught.'

The impressive thing about Joseph is that he thought about all those things before he made a mess of his life: 'I can't do this to Potiphar!' Most importantly of all, he remained faithful to his heavenly Master. Verse 9, he calls it 'a wicked thing . . . against God'. Here's the key reason Joseph stood up against temptation: for Joseph, God was the most important person in his life: 'How then could I do such a wicked thing and sin against God?' In putting God first, Joseph had this one overarching desire and passion that put all other passions in their place. Knowing God reorders all the loves of our heart.

The third way he overcame this temptation was – he distanced himself from sin: '. . . he refused to go to bed with her or even to be with her' (v. 10). Isn't that impressive? Joseph avoided all the situations where he might be alone with her.

If you find yourself attracted to someone who isn't your spouse, call it 'sin' and do not be alone with her or him. If you've got a problem with internet porn, call it what it is – it is lust. Put it into those terms, it will help you, call it what it is and then get a programme to limit your access to certain sites, or ask someone to be your accountability partner, where they will get a record of your internet activity.

Joseph called sin 'sin', he remained faithful to his master, he distanced himself from the situation. And, having done all those things, finally, he flees sin: 'She caught him by his cloak and said, "Come to bed with me!" But he left his cloak in her hand and ran out of the house' (v. 12). It is not a sign of weakness to run away. It actually takes a strong man to flee temptation.

All this is so important because Joseph, by doing this, could be trusted in the sexual arena. Joseph had overcome sin and now he could be trusted with leadership, where he would have women at his beck and call. Do you see why this was so significant? The more he overcame sin now, the more he could be trusted to overcome sin in the future. But the result of overcoming sexual sin is hardship.

Despair

In verses 16 to 20, it all goes downhill and so that leads, very briefly, to the third temptation of despair. Joseph had done everything right and everything had gone wrong and we're right back to where we started. When that happens, it's easy to despair and that's why we must believe that righteous living will bring suffering, and suffering does not mean that God has abandoned us. That is the pattern of the Christian life.

We're told here that the Lord was with Joseph. In Genesis 50:20, we know that God intended it all for good. And so, as you think of the ways that you have suffered for the gospel, consider this: if Joseph had not gone to prison, he'd never have met Pharaoh's chief cupbearer. He'd never have become the prince of Egypt. He'd never have then been used to save his family and thousands of others too. We have a perspective on Joseph's life that we don't have on our own lives.

This is written for our learning, for our own encouragement, so that when we are tempted to despair, we can look above our own life and know that there is a God who is controlling everything. When we've lived a right life and it has ended in suffering for us, we're to know God is with us, and that our standing against sin will help us to live for God in the future. In those times, we are to look to the ultimate Joseph, the one who was 'tempted in every way, just as we are – yet was without sin' (Heb. 4:15). The one who did nothing wrong, who was completely innocent and yet was wrongly accused and suffered at the hands of sinful men; the one who was despised and rejected; the one who suffered more than this Joseph ever did: he is the one whom God raised to life for the salvation of many.

To Egypt for the kingdom

by Steve Brady

Steve Brady

Steve Brady was born in Liverpool where he was converted in his teens, through a mixture of Bible reading and Everton football club. He is married with two children and three grandchildren. He has been in full-time Christian ministry for over thirty years, is Principal of Moorlands College and is a Trustee of Keswick Ministries. He holds a PhD degree in theology and is the author of *King of Heaven, Lord of Earth* and *All You Need Is Christ*, both Keswick Study Guides, to Colossians and Galatians respectively. A keen sportsman, he hates gardening and still has an irrational attachment to Everton football club.

To Egypt for the kingdom: Genesis 46:1–4,26–34; 47:1–12

Introduction

I suspect all of us have heard about the exodus, how the people of God eventually got out of Egypt. But why were they there? What were they doing there? Why this long, long, long narrative about the people of God, this nomadic tribe, making their way down into Egypt? What's it all about?

Of course at one level it's right and proper to read it and draw moral lessons about families and their success; things to avoid, their setbacks and failings and their restorations, their heroes and villains. We can approve or disapprove or sometimes try to work out what it is we're supposed to learn, but I think we've seen that behind these human stories is the story of God himself, of God working his purposes out.

So, as we turn the pages behind the narrative, there is this big story. And the big story is how God is going to save the world. The only trouble is, the weak human clay he's going to use is so fragile. So, if you were to go back to Genesis chapter 34, for instance, with these sons of Jacob, you'd be thinking twice about buying a second-hand car from any of them, if such were possible; you find there's a shocking narrative of what they did to the Shechemites, terrible, and then in chapter 35, the absolutely disgraceful behaviour of Reuben, the first-born, who slept with his father's concubine, Bilhah. And as a result, by chapter 48, that's what chapter 48's about, when Ephraim and Manasseh came, he is dislodged from being the first-born son. His sins do have temporal consequences and we need to remember that, don't we? It's so wonderful to know about forgiveness, but know this, that although we control our choices, we cannot control the consequences of our choices, and Reuben's folly, although forgiven, nevertheless had temporal implications. And then, of course, chapter 38 in particular is an outrageous story of male chauvinism – this guy Judah sleeping with a prostitute and then having the self-righteous audacity to be prepared to see his daughter-in-law, who'd already been widowed twice over, put to death because she was pregnant, only to discover that the twin boys in her womb had been placed there when he had impregnated her. It's a shocking, dreadful story, and it's wrapped round with the story of Joseph itself. This bunch of brothers who were potentially into fratricide: 'Let's kill our brother.' 'Oh no, let's not do that, let's get a few bob for him!'

Why do they need to go into Egypt? Answer: You've got it! Because they are so like the world around them they will never fulfil the purposes of God.

Isolated

There's a naivety around the church that if it were more like the world somehow we'd be attractive, when the whole history of the Bible and church history says it's when we are more like God in Christ that we're attractive. When we're like the world, who's interested in us?

The people of God were just like everybody else. And so God begins to move dramatically to take them out of their Canaanite culture so that he may take them into Egypt for one very simple reason – to isolate them from the culture. That's why the passage talks about them being shepherds; the Egyptians hated the shepherds (46:34) – why? Well, probably because many of them were town-dwellers and shepherds were nomads and often no-gooders. So they end up in the land of Goshen. Why? So that God can hermetically seal them off there, isolate them, quarantine them so that they can learn to be the people of God and fulfil the destiny for which he has created them.

And what is that destiny? Well, because this big story is running, it doesn't go back just to Abraham who was promised a great nation and a seed, it goes right back to the very dawn of creation when God looks at his spoilt world through our human rebellion but he promises, Genesis 3:15, that the seed of the woman will bruise the serpent's head. And then it's just down to eight with Noah, and he survives, and then it's Abraham and his seed and eventually, by the time we've got the whole panorama of Scripture, Galatians chapter 3 tells us who that seed really is: that seed is none other than Jesus Christ himself.

Why does God hermetically seal off, isolate, quarantine and preserve this bunch of villains? Because human clay is all he has got to work with. And unless his grace intervenes and he keeps this bunch of anti-heroes together and grows them into a people of God with Law and sacrifice and everything else, then eventually we have no big story, we have no Saviour of the world. And so, Joseph is the one who goes into a far country; he leaves his father's side, he goes into an alien country, so that others may follow him there. But that's not going to be the end of the process; in following Joseph into Egypt, they will ultimately follow him into a promised land.

What marks out a Christian is what's recorded in the book of Revelation chapter 14. They 'follow the Lamb wherever he goes' (v. 4). Christians are those who are followers, disciples; they follow the Lamb, and sometimes the Lamb leads them into strange places, takes them out of their comfort zone, takes them to places like Egypt – not Canaan, Egypt – for the kingdom. I wonder whether you've found your Egypt for the kingdom yet? I wonder whether you've worked out where you fit into the purposes of God?

Famine to shake us

There are some principles I think we can discern from these chapters. The first is simply this: 'Be ready.' God sometimes allows famine to shake us.

At the end of chapter 41, we read: 'And all the countries came to Egypt to buy grain from Joseph, because the famine was severe in all the world' (v. 57), and chapter 42, when Jacob learned there was grain in Egypt, he said to his sons, 'Why do you just keep looking at each other? . . . I have heard that there is grain in Egypt. Go down there and buy some for us, so that we may live and not die' (vv. 1,2). I like that. Jacob was the broken-hearted old guy, do you remember that? And yet here he is, twenty-odd years on, still calling the shots a bit. That's interesting, isn't it?

In the first church I served I had an old guy who enjoyed bad health. He was always dying and he wasn't that old; I suppose he was in the late sixties or more. One day I went round to see – let's call them Ted and Daisy – and while Daisy went out to make the tea, Ted was lying on the couch looking very glum, and he said, 'I'm going, chum, I'm going.' It was about another twenty years before he 'went'! All the last bit of Jacob's life, for the last twenty-odd years, he's been 'Going, chum, I'm going.' He's been dying, but he's still the patriarch and he says, 'Go down there and buy some [food] for us, that we may live and not die.' The purposes of God are not fulfilled in his life yet. But the days have become weeks, and the weeks months, and the months years, and he just, like many of us, feels like he's drifting through life. Where are the promises of God? When's the big thing that I'm supposed to do on planet Earth? When is it going to happen? The years have flown by. Then suddenly the famine comes. Famines are a wake-up call that life can't be the same again.

I wonder what your famine is, or is going to be? For some of us, of course, the easiest analogy is the credit crunch: we've suffered financial loss, we've lost our pension or our job. Or we've had a broken relationship, or a bereavement. One of the results of that is God is now using that famine for what he wants to do in us in the future. When we hit things that we don't like in the Christian life, rather than thinking to ourselves, 'Why, God, are you allowing this?' we need to know nothing happens behind our Father's back. The question is not 'Why me?' or 'Why this?' but 'Lord, what is it you are saying, and as a result, what is it you now want me to do?'

I remember a famine entering a friend of mine's life. It wasn't that serious but it was serious enough; he had to retire early from his teaching role. He was well compensated, and the result of this 'famine', as it were, was that suddenly he was free and the kids were off his hands and he and his wife were then able to go abroad and use their teaching skills and gifts in a mission school. The early retirement was his famine. Some of our students at Moorlands College have been given redundancy packages, and suddenly discovered that this is 'opportunity knocks'.

Caroline, Baroness Cox, was already a grandmother when she literally saw famines and injustices around the world. Suddenly, fifteen or more years ago, she sees this famine and it's a wake-up call to go do something different for Jesus. Are you facing your famine with 'Why me?'? Then be very careful; you may not get answers. But if it's 'Now Lord, what is it you want?' – as the eagle, it says in Deuteronomy 32:11, breaks up the nest, as God unsettles you, he knows what he's about; his purposes are on track. He's seeking to get your attention. God shakes us, usually before he makes us.

So be ready, God sometimes allows famine to shake us. But be glad! God often uses failure to break us, and grace to remake us.

Failure to break us

Jacob's is a highly dysfunctional family; they're a right mess. There are all sorts of sub-plots being played out with them, but by the time we get into chapter 42 and 44, having sold their brother off and being complicit in a wall of silence for a couple of decades, 'They said to one another, "Surely we are being punished because of our brother. We saw how distressed he was when he pleaded with us for his life, but we would not listen; that's why this distress has come upon us"' (42:21). And Reuben said, '"Didn't I tell you not to sin against the boy? But you wouldn't listen! Now we must give an accounting for his blood"' (v. 22). By the time we get to chapter 44, in one of the most poignant, moving passages in the whole of the Bible, there is Judah

> So now, if the boy is not with us when I go back to your servant my father and if my father, whose life is closely bound up with the boy's

life, sees that the boy isn't there, he will die. Your servants will bring the
grey head of our father down to the grave in sorrow. Your servant guaranteed the boy's safety to my father. I said, 'If I do not bring him back
to you, I will bear the blame before you, my father, all my life!' Now
then, please let your servant remain here as my lord's slave . . .
(vv. 30–33).

What has been going on with these guys? If you ever want to fix a
broken family, you've always got to wait for the famine. Forgiveness is
one thing but reconciliation is another. It takes time, and Joseph has
played this cat and mouse game with these guys because he wants to
discern that change has taken place in their hearts, that they are moving from their sinfulness and their arrogance and their failure so that
they can be used by God.

God does not use, for the evangelization of the world, super-saints
or archangels – he uses weak, Adamic clay. Failures. Sinners saved by his
grace – people like you and me. I was preaching somewhere recently
and I looked at things about the church and all its failings. I said, 'Some
of you are out there thinking, that's why I'm not a Christian, because
of all the failure and hypocrisy of the church.' And I said, 'The good
news is the church is for losers, so another one like you won't make
any difference. Come aboard!' They're the only kind of people who get
into the kingdom – and grace enables us to see ourselves.

At Moorlands, we have what we call our SPAR treatment, SPAR
– spiritual, practical, academic, relational. Spiritual – to shine for Jesus;
practical – training evangelists, youth workers, missionaries and whatever; academic, well, that's fairly straightforward. But the hardest part
is the 'r' bit, the relational element, and by that we mean where they
learn to bend and twist and get changed in the process of studying the
words of God so they don't come out of college as arrogant know-it-
alls. I often say to all the new students, 'Our task – myself and my col-
leagues, over the next three or four years – is to teach you so much
that at the end of it, you will realize how very, very, very little you
know.' We don't want to churn them out so they're mighty know-alls
as they get into ministry rather than being on the first rung – and that
self-knowledge is so important.

Some years ago I was in the States and I was down in Alistair Begg's church. One afternoon, he and I went down the gym. I hadn't run for a bit, but the gym had an interior running track, so while Alistair was on the running machine I was running round this track. And it was very good, it was an eighth of a mile exactly so eight times round you did a mile and you could time yourself, and it was one way. And as I was coming round the first bend I suddenly saw this fat old geezer running towards me. I thought, 'The poor old guy has got lost. Look at the state of him!' And then I realized it was me in the mirror.

God uses broken and fallen people. Alan Redpath spoke once about Stephen Olford. A young guy ran up to him as Stephen was getting on a plane, wanting to know the secret of serving the Lord. And Olford replied along the lines of, 'Bent knees, wet eyes, broken heart.'

Grace to remake us

These sons of Jacob are broken-hearted; the gospel tells us nobody need stay the way they are. That's what grace does. It may break us, but then it wants to remake us and shape us for the purposes of God. I was in full flow one morning in a church I served, and just making the point that God loves us so much that he receives us in Christ just as we are, when one of the most cantankerous of our members said, 'Thank God for that!' I hadn't finished. I said, 'And then he loves us too much to leave us as we are.' Followed by, thunderous – silence. That's the deal.

Grace wants to meet us where we are, and reconcile us to God. In the words of 2 Corinthians: 'God was reconciling the world to himself in Christ . . . We are therefore Christ's ambassadors, as though God were making his appeal through us. We implore you on Christ's behalf: Be reconciled to God. God made him who had no sin to be sin for us, so that in him we might become the righteousness of God' (vv. 19–21). God bears with our human failure; God bears with our folly, that he might redeem it. And if you or I are to find our Egypt for God, then some of us maybe need a breaking as well as a shaking;

some of us are just too proud and 'together' to be useful to the Master.

Be ready, God sometimes allows famine to shake us; be glad, God often uses failure to break us, and grace to remake us.

Faith to take us

But finally therefore be available, for God always demands faith to take us; in the words of the best split infinitive in history: 'To boldly go.' Faith will always take you where you've never been before. You do not need faith in the Christian life to stay where you are or how you are; just drift along, just have a nice day, just keep the machinery ticking over, just go through the motions. But you will never be changed and you'll never know the incredible thrill and exhilaration of knowing that you're walking in the purposes of God.

If you want to stay where you are, stay well away from the rest of this message. Because what I am about to say could seriously damage your spiritual well-being; it could mess your life up and take you into the vast exciting purposes of God for your life. It could take you to Egypt and you just wanted to stay in Bridlington.

Out of the comfort zone

Chapter 45:28 says this: 'Israel said, "I'm convinced! My son Joseph is still alive. I will go and see him before I die."' And then in chapter 46 it seems like he gets cold feet: 'So Israel set out with all that was his . . . And God spoke to Israel in a vision at night and said, "Jacob! Jacob!" "Here I am," he replied. "I am God, the God of your father . . . Do not be afraid to go down to Egypt . . ."' (vv. 1–3).

Don't be afraid! Why should he be afraid? Where's that from? Probably because of something his old dad reminded him of. In chapter 26, God said to Isaac, 'Do not go down to Egypt; live in the land where I tell you to live' (v. 2). Now God is saying, 'Hey! Forget what your old man said. I want you to go where I told your father not to go.'

At one level it was a nice providential coincidence; by going down to Egypt he would see his long-lost boy, the family would be secure, he'd have a place to live in the famine years . . . but he was going there because God wanted him to go. The Lord turned up in a dramatic way in a vision to say, 'It's Egypt for you now, Jacob.'

I've heard thousands of sermons over the forty or so years I've been a Christian. I remember over thirty years ago hearing a guy who took just ten minutes. He took that verse from Revelation 2, in the King James version it reads: 'I know . . . where thou dwellest', Revelation 2:13, the church of Pergamum: 'I know where you live – where Satan has his throne.' And he just rammed home the message: God knows where you are. God knows your address. God knows why he wants you there or wants to move you on. And when God wants to move us on and we refuse and say no, we are always the losers. We are a pilgrim people, we are called as Christians to be kingdom of God seekers first of all; not 'How will this affect my career? How will this affect my family?' but 'How will this move affect my family and the family of God?' And here's the rub. God calls this whole family out of its comfort zone, into Egypt.

Of course the Egyptians themselves are blessed by that. They say, 'You have saved our lives through Joseph' (see 47:25). When God's people are in God's place there's always blessing around, even for those who are not believers. And as we've noted, they're hermetically sealed off in this land of Goshen, because Joseph had primed them to tell Pharaoh, 'Your servants have tended livestock from our boyhood on, just as our fathers did' (46:34), so in chapter 47:6, Pharaoh says, 'Let them live in Goshen. And if you know of any among them with special ability, put them in charge of my own livestock.' Why are they there? Because, as I intimated, they're away from pagan influences, they're away from the towns and everything else where worship of other gods goes on, because God has got a purpose in moving them to Egypt. He's already sent ahead a saviour figure. Others join this saviour in a strange land so that, one day, through this people they may come to a promised land. Does that ring any bells? And he calls his people out of their comfort zones, in the words of an old book by Michael Griffiths, 'to give up our small ambitions' and to be a pilgrim people, a people on the move, a people who, as we read in Hebrews 11, are looking for a city whose Builder and Maker is God.

Do you notice who makes this move? Some of you are sitting there thinking, 'It's all right for you, Steve, but I'm an old geezer now.' I've got some great news for you. Do you know how old Jacob was when the call came, 'Go to Egypt!'? He was 130 years old. At 130 years of age, he is called to a significant ministry. Maybe God's going to call you out of your home and he's going to put you in sheltered accommodation or a nursing home and you're thinking, 'That's the end of the world.' No it isn't, because where you will reside there will be flights getting called every day. And you're in the departure lounge, and your task is to make sure that you can talk to others so that when their flight is called, they've got the ticket to get on the right plane to go to heaven. Maybe that's going to be your Egypt and you're going to find that it's going to lead many to the Promised Land.

As I go through this narrative I find that there are mature people too that are the leaders of tribes, the sons of Reuben and Simeon and so on; these are guys who've been through the famine, the credit crunch, the early retirement, and they're sensing God's call to Christian service. God is calling some of us in our middle years to say, 'Right, you've done that. Now for something really big.' Don't keep putting it off if it's your famine that's got your attention. And there are sons of sons here, aren't there, the sons of Judah, and Issachar, and Benjamin, younger people called out of their nomadic lives in the saving purposes of God.

One of my great privileges is chatting to all the new students who come, hearing their stories of faith. Some of them come from great Christian homes and we need to keep thanking God for that because they're often kept from gross and evil sin. It's a wonderful thing when you can say like Obadiah in the book of Kings, 'I have worshipped the LORD since my youth' (see 1 Kgs. 18:12). And many of us have been called to serve the Lord Jesus in our younger days.

The cost

God takes them, taking their shepherd skills, taking what's in their hands, like he says in Exodus 4 to Moses, 'What's in your hand?' 'It's a staff.' God wants to take what's in your hand – your financial skills, your legal skills, your medical skills, your teaching skills, your gift of help skills, ready for anything for Jesus skills, your listening and compassionate heart skills – to open doors for his purposes of grace.

God wants to grow his people in some strange locations, like Goshen. Only, how are you going to get there? I like the end of chapter 45, 'when he saw the carts Joseph had sent . . . the spirit of their father Jacob revived' (v. 27). 'Joseph has sent you the carts! Jacob, your chariot awaits!' You see, when the King of kings wants you to go, how you're going to get there is his responsibility, right? And if he's going to send you a cart or a handcart – or a Zimmer – then he'll do so.

You say, 'It is costly to go, Steve.' If the Lord's speaking to you, if you stay where you are you'll die of starvation as surely as Jacob and his family would have done.

I was saved when I was just sixteen. One of the first books I read was Elisabeth Elliot's *Shadow of the Almighty* and I started work in local government, just as a fill-in job, ready to go to Bible college, writing to mission societies, 'When can I come?' 'When you've grown up, son.'

In the summer of 1971, God just seemed to be pestering the daylights out of me by a whole pile of 'coincidences', and eventually I wrote to London Bible College. I'd written to them when I was eighteen and I was now writing when I was twenty. I came home Tuesday 14 September 1971 and there was a letter: 'Doubtless you were thinking of applying to come to London Bible College next year.' Yeah, oh yeah, it's good . . . because by this time I'd been promoted, I was the boss's blue-eyed boy, I was loving what I was doing, I was really settled . . . 'But we have vacancies for the course commencing 30 September 1971.'

Well, that was easy, it was a no-brainer. I had to give a month's notice and I hadn't got any finance and . . . and all these excuses started gabbling out. I had one of the most miserable and memorable nights of my life. I remember going into my bedroom, getting down on my knees and wrestling like I'd never wrestled before in prayer saying, 'God, I can't go. I haven't got the money to go. I can't leave work now. I can't leave me ma!' And suddenly this whole sense of voices, 'Think of the sacrifice, son!' All of these dark things and I'm thinking, 'I can't go' when a light from heaven shone into my soul. The

Lord reminded me of One who left his Father's side, gave up all the privileges of being the co-equal, co-eternal Son of God to come and rescue people like me. I can remember in that most moving, life-changing experience, saying, simply, 'Lord, I am willing, but you've got to make it possible.' Within twenty-four hours the boss was on my side; within two weeks I was starting as a student at London Bible College, training for a lifetime in Christian ministry.

I thought of all this I was giving up, sacrifice. Sacrifice? I don't think I even know how to spell it, walking with Jesus. I've given nothing up. All I've given up is my tight-fisted hanging on to what I've got. Letting go, your hands are open – I have received far, far, far more than I can ever remunerate: the incalculable blessings of God in Jesus Christ. I'm so grateful for a night I will never forget.

How about you?

All our Lord needs is your willingness. Gladys Aylward, nobody would have her, on her knees with a Bible, all her money – two sixpences, five pence – and she says, 'Lord, here's my Bible, here's my money and here's me. Please take and use me.' Boy, did God use her. It's not great gifts and great talents God uses; it's great availability and willingness to say yes to Jesus even if it's Egypt, even if it's out of our comfort zone, because life is too short if the Lord is calling us.

In a week when we remember one small step for man, one giant leap for mankind, God, I believe, is calling us, young and old and middle-aged, to take one small step out of our comfort zones for the kingdom of God, and his glory.

Abraham, the father of faith

by John Risbridger

John Risbridger

John Risbridger works as Minister and Team Leader at Above Bar Church, in Southampton. After five years in hospital management, he spent ten years working with UCCF – first as a regional team leader and then as Head of Student Ministries. He still has a passion for student work and is involved in university missions and various student training events. John has served as a Trustee of Keswick Ministries for a number of years. He is married to Alison and they have two daughters. John loves walking (and eating cream teas) in the New Forest with his wife and family. His other interests include current affairs and listening to music of all kinds.

Abraham, the father of faith: Hebrews 11:8–12, 17–19

Introduction

Taking God at his word

I work in a church in Southampton called Above Bar Church. A few years ago, there was too much going on in church life for those of us on the staff to handle, so we decided that we were going to appoint a church manager. We gave the job to a young guy called Chris, and he is absolutely fantastic. He's completely unflappable, he's efficient, but the thing that I really love about Chris is that he is a man of his word. You can take him at his word, and you can depend on what he says.

We're looking at Abraham and the faith of Abraham. Abraham was the man that the apostle Paul in Romans 4:11 calls 'the father of all who believe' – hence the title this evening, 'Abraham, the father of faith'. He's the figure that the whole Bible looks back to as the great model of faith.

The writer of Hebrews 11 uses this little phrase 'By faith' to describe Abraham four times in this passage. If you look through them, you'll see that on each occasion that we're told 'by faith' Abraham did something, on each occasion Abraham is taking God at his word. On three of the four occasions you'll read specifically that he is believing the promises of God.

Hebrews 11 is about the faith that God commends. Did you notice that, verse 2? 'This is what the ancients were commended for' and then go right to the end of the passage, verse 39, 'These were all commended for their faith'. Hebrews 11 is about the faith that God commends. What is the faith that God commends? It's the faith that takes God at his word; that believes his promises. So we're going to look at each of the 'by faiths' in Abraham's life as Hebrews 11 records them.

Faith to leave (v. 8)

The first is in verse 8 and it's faith to leave: 'By faith Abraham, when called to go to a place he would later receive as his inheritance, obeyed and went, even though he did not know where he was going.' It is recording that very foundational moment in the Old Testament, in Genesis chapter 12 where the Lord said to Abraham: 'Leave your country, your people and your father's household and go to the land I will show you' (v. 1). The writer of Hebrews 11 is picking up on that last phrase, 'I will show you.' He went even though he didn't know where he was going.

Abraham was going to an unknown land in an unknown place, but still he set out in the obedience to the commands of God. The place he left behind was Ur of the Chaldeans, one of the cradles of civilization in the ancient world, and as he set out from there he left his family, his security, everything that he'd known; he left civilization itself and began the journey to Canaan. If you read the accounts in Genesis you'll realize that there were some hiccups and delays along the way, but the emphasis here in Hebrews 11 is on the immediacy of his response to the word of God. You could translate it, 'even as he was called, Abraham obeyed and went'. He knows you can depend on the word of God, and he acts in obedience.

It's astonishing when you think of it, isn't it? This is a great moment in the whole of the Bible story. From this moment it's going to open up first from a man, then to a family, then to a nation, then to all the nations receiving the blessing of God. And it all starts here in the story of this one man who hears the call of God and obeys that call; this one man who has faith to leave.

Some of us coming to Keswick this year know that God has been calling us to leave in some way; maybe he's calling us on to a new ministry, calling us to a new job – perhaps we've lost the old job and we don't yet know what the new job is, a little bit like Abraham here. Maybe it's a new role in our church, all kinds of different possibilities. God is calling us to leave, but we don't know quite where to yet. We don't know quite what the shape is of what he's calling us on to. Abraham stands as the great example of someone who believes the word of God and obeys, even though he doesn't understand. If you're at one of those turning points in your life, I just want to encourage you to take Abraham's faith as your model and to embrace the future that God leads you on to. Maybe you don't know the details. Abraham didn't either, but God does. Have faith to leave.

To the first readers of Hebrews 11, this whole idea of leaving in response to God's command probably had a rather more specific reference. Hebrews was written to a predominantly Jewish congregation of Christians, a group of people who'd had to come to terms with the fact that God had spoken a new word to human beings in Jesus Christ, that God had established a new covenant with human beings in the blood of Jesus Christ, and that they had therefore been called to leave the old way of their ancestors with its laws and rituals, and now had to embrace the new covenant way of freedom in Christ. They had needed faith to leave, and the great challenge in Hebrews is that many of them were beginning to want to turn back. They needed faith to leave and faith to keep on leaving, not to turn back, even though they were tempted to.

Obeying the call

The chances are that if you've been coming to Keswick for a number of years, you have heard that call to leave on many occasions. Maybe you heard it as the call to leave a life of selfishness and materialism and give all that you are and all that you have to Jesus and for the gospel. Maybe you heard it as a call to leave a life of self-made success and pride, and to acknowledge that you need Jesus to meet your deepest needs. Maybe it was a call to leave a life of atheism or agnosticism from which God is excluded, or at least pushed to the margins, and you're called to leave and embrace the life of faith. It's one thing to hear the call of God, but Abraham's challenge to us is that just hearing it is not sufficient; have you *obeyed* the call of God? Have you left that way of life and embraced the life of faith in Jesus Christ? You may say, 'I've still got questions.' I've still got questions! Every honest believer has still got questions. Abraham still had questions. The call isn't to get all our questions answered. The call is to hear the voice of God and to obey. Have you left? Are you following? We all have our faith in something. Is yours in God and his word?

Faith to stay (vv. 9,10)

In verses 9 and 10 we've got another 'By faith', and you could say this is about faith to stay. 'By faith [Abraham] made his home in the promised land like a stranger in a foreign country; he lived in tents, as did Isaac and Jacob, who were heirs with him of the same promise. For he was looking forward to the city with foundations, whose architect and builder is God.' Verse 9 doesn't go as you expect it to, does it? The first bit's fine: 'By faith he made his home in the promised land'. He had faith to stay in the place God had led him to, but how did he stay there? You expect it to finish something like this, don't you – 'By faith he made his home in the promised land and there he settled and prospered and everything was lovely.' What you find instead is that there in the promised land he lived 'like a stranger in a foreign country', end of verse 9. This status as a stranger in a foreign land wasn't just a temporary thing while Abraham settled in: for him, it was a lifestyle.

Did you see verse 9 in the middle there, 'he lived in tents'? I want to say to you, I like that verse a lot because I'm living in a tent in Keswick this week. Abraham was a camper, he lived in tents. It was an expression of his faith. I can tell you it took quite a bit of faith to be a camper in Keswick last night, with the rain lashing down on the tents! Why are we camping? Why didn't we just buy a house in Keswick? Well, there are some fairly obvious reasons why we didn't buy a house in Keswick, to do with ministerial salaries and all that, but actually the reason that we're camping is because Keswick isn't our home. We're just visitors, temporary residents, which is why we're in the tents.

That is why Abraham remained in a tent in the Promised Land. The Promised Land remained a foreign country to Abraham. Why? Because, verse 10, 'he was looking forward to the city with foundations, whose architect and builder is God.' This is crucial. We can easily misunderstand what is being said here, as if this is all just about the journey to Canaan. What we're actually being told is that the journey to Canaan was part of a much bigger journey that Abraham was on; he wasn't just looking for the Promised Land as an earthly place. His heart was for a heavenly city, the city with foundations. Bill Lane, one of the commentators on this passage, says that the tents 'showed that Abraham was unwilling to establish a permanent settlement in a culture devoid of the presence of God.'[1] Have you got that? Unwilling to establish a permanent residence in a culture devoid of the presence of God!

Two questions

Verses 13 to 16 seemed to interrupt the story of Abraham, did you notice? There's more about Abraham afterwards in verses 17 to 19 that we'll look at a little bit later. Why do those verses interrupt the story? Was it just a little afterthought? Not at all. This is the key to understanding Abraham's faith; this is to help us see that the Promised Land pointed to something *beyond* the Promised Land. The real goal of Abraham's journey was not the Promised Land, but the heavenly city of God – what we as New Testament Christians know as the New Jerusalem, which will come down out of heaven from God when Jesus returns in all his glory to renew creation and make it his home.

I've got two questions I want you to think about. The first is this: What do you think is really real? Is it that there's a real world down here with rocks and water and mountains and concrete, and then there's this floaty, surreal, spiritual world of shadows and vagueness in heaven where one day we hope we'll be, and dream happy thoughts for ever? Is that the way it is? The real world's here, and it's a shadowy world there? I think many of us think that way. But see how Abraham's faith turns all of that on its head; verse 10, 'he was looking forward to the city with foundations'. Do you see the contrast? There he is living in flippy-floppy tents held up by guy ropes and pegs, and he's looking forward to the city with foundations, solid, real, lasting. For Abraham, the really real world was the world to come; what we would call the new creation or perhaps better, the renewed creation; creation 'liberated', as Paul says in Romans 8:21, 'from its bondage to decay' and impermanence; creation as the dwelling place again of God as he comes to live with his people. That's the really real world – that's what's worth living for. In comparison, we're living in a world of shadows now. As one translation puts verse 1: 'faith perceives the things we hope for, as objectively real and the things we have not yet seen as certain'.

Do you need to turn your thinking upside down? Get rid of vague notions of heaven and embrace the joy of the new creation in all its solidness, in all its richness, in all the vibrancy of its hope and life. What do you think is really real?

The second question is: Do you seem like an alien? I don't mean do you look green and slimy, and occasionally go 'bleep' to signal your alien status. What I mean instead is, are you living as a temporary resident in this age, because you've invested your hopes in the age to come? Is it obvious that that's the way that you and I are living? I'm not talking about retreating from society into a little escapist huddle with a faith which Os Guinness once described as 'privately engaging but socially irrelevant'. I'm talking about living in this world, in its realities, but with eternity's values in view and driving all your decisions. C.S. Lewis once said that if you read history, you would find that the Christians who did the most in the present world were the ones who thought the most about the next world.

That's real Christian living. Do you seem like an alien? Are your ambitions set by the approval of your boss, by the status gains of society, or by the desire to please your real Master, and being ready to give an account to him? What about your possessions? Are they, in fact, your master? Or are they invested to produce a return in eternity? Are you living for things, or for people and for God? What about your politics? Are your politics shaped merely by self-interest or by unquestioning loyalty to party or to nation, or are they shaped by God's passion for righteousness and justice in the world? Is it clear that you're an alien, that you're operating by different principles and values? Suppose you were put in court, accused of being a citizen of heaven. Would there be the evidence to convict you?

Faith to believe the impossible (vv. 11,12)

Then in verses 11 and 12, we've got faith to believe the impossible. Have you noticed how many of the key moments in the Bible story seem to turn on the agonizing pain of a couple without children? It was that way in Abraham's story: turn to Genesis chapter 15: 'After this, the word of the LORD came to Abram in a vision: "Do not be afraid, Abram. I am your shield, your very great reward"' (Gen. 15:1). It's a wonderful promise that God had made to him saying that his protection would not come from military strength but from God himself – 'I am your shield.' His reward would not be the wealth of Sodom that he had just rejected in chapter 14, his reward would be God himself. Having God, what else could he desire in heaven or on earth? That's enough. 'Your reward is me.' A wonderful promise. But even though Abraham is a great model of faith, he's a model of honest faith. And so Genesis 15:2: Abraham said, '"O Sovereign LORD, what can you give me since I remain childless and the one who will inherit my estate is Eliezer of Damascus?"' Can't you feel the pain in that question? Can't you feel the echoes of years of disappointment, of weary days of dashed hopes again? For those of us who have perhaps asked similar questions of God, surely we can at least take comfort from the fact that this man, whom the Bible portrays as the model of faith, was nonetheless the man who questioned God in this way. It is clear from Abraham that true faith can, at times, be perplexed and questioning faith.

One of the things I most love about the Bible is hearing words spoken to God by us which are uncomfortable and questioning and challenging – but God has put them in his word. Why? I think to give us permission to ask the same questions of God when our lives are full of pain and questions and uncertainty.

What was God's response? 'Then the word of the LORD came to him: "This man [Eliezer of Damascus] will not be your heir, but a son coming from your own body will be your heir." He took him outside and said, "Look up at the heavens and count the stars – if indeed you can count them." Then he said to him, "So shall your offspring be"' (Gen. 15:4,5). Isn't that stunning? Now every time that Abraham peered out of his tent and looked up to a star-studded sky, he would remember the promise of God. But was it a believable promise? Humanly speaking, the answer was no; it wasn't a believable promise. Abraham was old, Sarah was unable to have children. So it didn't seem a believable promise, but how did Abraham respond? 'Abram believed the LORD, and he credited it to him as righteousness' (Gen. 15:6). It may have been impossible but it was not in the end unbelievable, because God had promised it. Faith to believe the impossible; and that, of course, is the point that Hebrews 11 picks up the end of verse 11: Abraham 'was enabled to become a father because he considered him faithful who had made the promise.'

Faith to believe the impossible. Faith to be certain of what he could not see. Not because he was a generally optimistic person, but because God had spoken and, by faith, he believed the promise. Abraham saw that neither his past experience nor his present circumstances had the final power to determine his destiny. Only God possesses that power. And let me say in your life, only God possesses the power to determine your destiny, and it is of the nature of faith to recognize that.

Abraham didn't live to see the fulfilment that God had in store in its fullness, but just look at what came from it, verse 12: 'from this one man, and he as good as dead, came descendants as numerous as the stars in the sky and as countless as the sand on the seashore.'

A problem

It would, I think, be cruel to try to apply this passage in a way that suggested that God will always give us the child for which we long, the relationship we've hoped for, the job we're seeking, if only we have the faith that God will always deliver. Some of us carry huge burdens and are facing impossible and agonizing situations. God has promised his grace to help us and his presence to comfort us, and surely we can't read the story of Abraham without having our faith rekindled and encouraged that sometimes God does help us in extraordinary ways, in powerful ways, in unexpected ways, but don't you also sometimes find the kind of 'happy endings' in the Bible a bit of a problem?

I was talking a while ago to a man who'd lost his wife. We were talking about Job, and he said to me, 'The trouble is, it feels like the book of Job gets spoiled by the ending where it all works out again. My life hasn't had the happy ending.' I want to say to you, my life hasn't always had happy endings. There are unanswered questions for me as well. But I found it helpful to reflect on the fact that the 'happy endings' in the Bible seem to me very, very often to point beyond themselves. Surely that's the case here, isn't it? Yes, Abraham's story did have the happy ending – Isaac was born. But Isaac's birth was the beginning of something so much greater, as we saw in verse 12, this great harvest; and we are part of that harvest, because the children of Abraham are not only the biological descendants, they are all the   people of faith, Jew and Gentile, across the world. So Abraham's happy ending was pointing forward to a happy ending for the whole of humanity, ultimately, that will embrace Jew and Gentile; a happy ending in which each of us can share. That, of course, doesn't take away the pain of disappointment. It doesn't answer all the questions. But in my experience, it has at times brought great hope when I might otherwise have been overwhelmed by despair.

Most of us live in a nation where the Christian church seems weak and often defeated, and I want to suggest that there is a fresh need for us to believe the impossible. Jesus has promised to build his church, and it seems to me increasingly clear that God looks for a people who will still believe the impossible and will keep on praying that God will revive his church again.

Faith to sacrifice the most valuable (vv. 17–19)

Finally, faith to sacrifice the most valuable. 'By faith Abraham, when God tested him, offered Isaac as a sacrifice' (v. 17). This surely was the greatest test of faith. Of course, there was all the emotional agony that any parent would experience in being called to sacrifice their own child, but that wasn't all; when Abraham had left his homeland, God had asked him to say goodbye to his past. But here he is being asked to say goodbye to his future as well, because remember that it was through Isaac that God had said the promises were going to be fulfilled, those promises of a future countless offspring.

Now, God had no intention of letting the sacrificial knife actually fall. Child sacrifice has always been abhorrence to God. And yet there was a real sense in which in the heart of Abraham the offering had already been made before the knife fell. He'd made the decision, in his heart he had offered him up, (v. 17) he 'offered Isaac as a sacrifice.' Why? The writer tells us it was because his confidence in the promise of God was so strong that he knew that not even death could keep that promise from being fulfilled.

With that same hope in the resurrection now brilliantly lit up and illuminated for us through the resurrection of Jesus from the dead, we too are called, and indeed freed, to sacrifice even the most valuable for God as Abraham did by faith, because he believed in the resurrection. For those of us who might imagine that this means sacrificing our children on the altar of ecclesiastical ambition, let's remember that's not the point; God is still against child sacrifice. But as parents, if you are a parent, what about the challenge of releasing our children – or indeed, other loved ones – to follow God's purpose for them, wherever it may take them, and however painful it may be for us to cope with that? Or for others of us, what about giving up to God our most cherished ambition, our most cherished dreams, until our only one ambition is to please him and bear fruit for his glory? Is this your faith? Is this my faith – faith to believe the impossible? Faith to sacrifice the most valuable?

Another Father, another Son

Before we leave this story of a father called to sacrifice his son on a hill in ancient times, let's just move our focus again; move our focus to another hill – the hill of Calvary, on which another Father offered another Son, his one and only Son, because the God who promised Abraham that he would provide an offering, himself became an offering in the Person of his Son, Jesus Christ.

Consider the faith of Jesus, faith to leave – he left the glory. The Word who was with the Father from all eternity, came and made his dwelling, set up his tent, stayed among us. Consider the faith of Jesus going to the cross, laying down his life, believing that in making that sacrifice he would be providing the ransom that would set many free. Consider the faith of Jesus Christ giving even himself, offering the most valuable for the fulfilment of God's purpose and for his glory in the world. As Jesus hung on the cross, bearing our sins on his shoulders, the sacrificial knife did fall; there was no other offering needed because this was the one offering in all history that really counted. The knife fell and Jesus the Son of God took into himself the very wrath of God against all our sins, so that it might never fall on us. Having suffered under the weight of our sins, this Son, Jesus, was raised from the dead, defeating death in his resurrection and guaranteeing eternal life for all of us who trust him.

Abraham's faith was faith in the promise of God. But the promises that Abraham believed find their true fulfilment not in Isaac, but in Jesus Christ, the one great Son of the Father, and it's therefore by placing our faith in him, in Jesus, that we truly make Abraham's faith our own.

Is that your faith?

The faith that God commends is faith to leave – have you heard that call? To leave everything and follow Jesus, as his disciple – have you obeyed that call? It's faith to stay, it's faith to live as a resident alien in the present age, because our lives are already submitted to the King of the age to come. Faith to leave, faith to stay; it's faith to believe the impossible, that in the kingdom of which Jesus Christ is the King there is certain hope for a broken world and a guarantee of eternal life for us. And it's faith to sacrifice the most valuable, because to know King Jesus and to belong to his kingdom is to know the pearl of great price for which we gladly give up all things. Is that your faith?

Faith in leadership – Moses

by Stephen Gaukroger

Stephen Gaukroger

Stephen Gaukroger has been a senior pastor for 26 years. He was President of the Baptist Union of Great Britain 1994–5, and is on the Council of Management for Spring Harvest. He is now the Founder-Director of Clarion Trust International. It is clear through his teaching and the impact of his life that he regards mission/evangelism as a key priority for the church. His firm grasp of our postmodern culture is evident as he addresses its challenges with an unquestioned commitment to Scripture. Through conferences, councils, books and CDs, his ministry has affected the nation. Over the last five years, Stephen has had opportunities to speak to Christian leaders and to engage in evangelism in over twenty countries worldwide.

Faith in leadership – Moses: Hebrews 11:23–29

Introduction

Moses is one of those characters that towers over the Old Testament literature. Indeed, for Jews, it's hard to think of an equal character. Certainly Abraham was incredibly significant, and later King David was to be someone from whom Jesus would ultimately come, but many would say that Moses, above all, because of the giving of the Law, was the significant character. Indeed, there's a huge body of Jewish literature that points to Moses as an incredible commander, a warrior, a leader of Egyptian troops. There are some Jewish stories about him in the period up to the age of forty when he seems to have made this transition into rebellion – as far as the Egyptians would have understood it – in which he was very significantly expanding the empire of the pharaoh by his military activity.

What faith is

There is a school of thought that Moses was actually the inventor of the alphabet, taken from the ancient Egyptians, via the Phoenicians, through to the Greeks and ultimately down into our own alphabet – fascinating insights. I've no idea of the exact veracity of these tales but they point to a man of enormous significance and there are a number of incidents in his life in Hebrews 11. But I want to preface it by making sure that we've grappled a little bit more with what faith is. Because by faith we're going to think about Moses' parents doing an amazingly brave thing, and Moses himself entering into their courage and living out a very distinctive lifestyle, when he could have had all the joys of being Pharaoh's daughter's son. We're going to see the miracle of the day when there was incredibly awful death among the first-born of Egypt, but the first-born of Israel survived because of this Passover lamb that was slain. Then ultimately we're going to be seeing this great deliverance from captivity across the Sea of Reeds, sometimes called the Red Sea. So it is a staggering story, and it's all by faith.

Faith is notoriously difficult to define. Hebrews chapter 11:1 is an attempt at a definition but, for many western minds, it's quite slippery. The sort of related theological concepts in the New Testament are words like 'trust' or 'belief' or 'believe', even 'faithfulness' – the sort of extended version of faith.

Faith is not a feeling. That's very important because sometimes people say, 'I've really got faith for this.' People use that kind of expression and I'm never quite sure what they mean. Do they mean 'I really feel good about this'? Imagine preparing to come to Keswick and saying to your wife or husband, 'I have a really good feeling about Keswick this year. I'm full of faith. Let's just pack shorts and skimpy tops. Let's leave the umbrella at home. Let's forget the coats. It's going to be great! I have real faith for that.' Let's say you said that and let's say you shared that with your husband or wife and with your children and they all agreed together that they felt that was right. And you arrived with your suntan lotion ready . . . However much faith you had, in that sense, however much of a feeling that you thought things would be all right – it would have turned out to be misplaced faith!

Faith is not a feeling we have to drum up. Sometimes people talk about praying, particularly in a healing context, 'If only we had enough feeling of faith, something might happen. Perhaps we could even twist God's arm into turning up and doing something.' That's not what the Bible means by faith. It's not the amount of faith. Indeed faith itself is quite difficult to describe. We probably have to go to some of the things that Jesus said, for example, 'By their fruit you will recognize them' (Matt. 7:16). In other words, you sometimes can't quite work out what faith is, apart from the consequences of faith – what you see faith produce. For example, you could say, 'It's windy here.' Someone else will say, 'I can't feel the wind on my face or blowing my hair about, my umbrella's fine, I don't see the trees moving, there are no slamming of doors.' In other words, you're not going to believe there's a strong wind unless the evidence of it is around; you can't see it, but you see signs of its presence. So faith is not a matter of quantity. Jesus said, 'If you had the faith of a mustard seed, you could move a mountain' (see Matt. 17:20). It's the object of the faith which is central. We can drum up as much faith as we want in something, but it will be foolishness and presumption if the object of our faith is flimsy, inadequate and failing.

So, right at the start, we have to understand that when we say 'Moses did things by faith', it is not a feeling of spirituality or a warm glow about God. It is an inner conviction that the promises of God can be relied upon and ultimately acted upon. And so we see the faith of Moses – and the book of James expounds this for us so thoroughly – we see the faith of Moses in what he chose to do in response to the promises of God. Not what he chose to *feel* but how he chose to *act* – and, for some of you, you need to hear that. You'll be so relieved that you don't have to feel spiritual for God to bless you.

The fruit of faith

So, we recognize that faith is something that is demonstrated by its consequences and is difficult to define. Theologians have argued about this for a very long time. We look for the consequences – or, as Jesus said, the 'fruit' – of faithful living. And you notice, if you just look through the passage, that some kind of verb or some kind of activity follows the 'By faith' phrase. Verse 23: 'By faith Moses' parents *hid* him' (emphasis added). They did something in response to what they thought of as God's plan. 'By faith Moses, when he had grown up, *refused* to be known' (v. 24, emphasis added) – he did something on the basis of what he thought was right. 'By faith he *left* Egypt' (v. 27, emphasis added); 'by faith, he *kept* the Passover' (v. 28, emphasis added); 'by faith, the people passed' (v. 29, my italics) – they did something.

Although faith isn't a work, it's not something we bring to Jesus in some kind of transaction – sometimes people have made that mistake; they think that salvation is that God brings his love in Jesus Christ, we bring our faith and a kind of contract takes place – we've done our bit and he does his bit – whereas we know, from the wider scriptural revelation, that salvation is all of God, *all* of him, and that faith is not something we have to drum up. But what we have to do is not to *feel* something but, in response to the promises of God, to *act* in a particular way; to act in a way that demonstrates this faith, a way of holiness, a way of righteousness, a way of truthfulness, a way of honour and integrity. That's what God's looking for from the church of Jesus in our nation; women and men who trust him, take him at his word, put their confidence, bet their life – if I could put it crudely – that he's honest and true and right and just and he's really God. And, 'I'll put my weight on that reality, I'll trust his word, I'll act as if it's true.' That's faith, to see that worked out. So we've got to do something to get on board with God.

Most of us exercise faith almost every day. Faith – taking a step and acting on what we know to be right, putting our confidence in something that's reliable. I'm a fearful flyer. I fly a lot actually – usually by plane – and I'm nervous as a flyer. People say to me, 'Steve, are you afraid of flying?' And I say, 'No, of course not. I'm afraid of *not* flying!' Because I'm a nervous flyer, I watch people on aeroplanes. I've been told the planes are perfectly safe. I've had the aerodynamics explained to me by so many people I've lost track: large engines, aerodynamic shape, the thing takes off. But I watch nervous people on aeroplanes, and they're just like me; they fidget with their safety belt, they look around nervously, they put their hands on the armrest and then fiddle with their belt again and they're the only people who are paying attention to the safety briefing. And then the plane sets off down the runway and you're forced back in your seat. And you watch, next time you're flying, the nervous people, they grab the armrests, stare straight ahead and, as that amazing moment comes when the nose wheel comes up and the back comes off the ground, they rise out of their seat and there's daylight underneath their bottoms because they're helping the plane off the ground.

I don't know how those big metal things get in the air, I don't know how they stay there. People can talk to me all they want about aerodynamics and I can say, 'I believe you, I believe you, I believe it'll fly but, until I trust my weight to it and my body to that plane, my words mean nothing.' An action has to demonstrate a statement of belief and faith. We can say, 'We love Jesus and want to follow him' all we want, but we have to have the fruit of faith.

Faith overcomes fear (vv. 23, 27)

So that's what's going on here. By faith, something happens. What is it? Firstly, we see faith defeating fear. Look with me at verse 23: 'By faith Moses's parents hid him' and this is, by the way, Moses's parents exercising faith 'after he was born, because they saw he was no ordinary child'. Almost all the commentators say that it's not that he was somehow very attractive. Newborn babies aren't very attractive, usually. I know I'm probably offending people now but I think all newborn babies look like Winston Churchill, they're just crushed and squidgy. So it's not that; I don't think they thought, 'Moses, oh, how lovely!' – I mean, I'm sure his mother did. But they somehow sensed – because this story's repeated not just in Exodus but picked up by Stephen in his sermon in the Acts of the Apostles – that there was 'something' about this child. God's hand was on it. There seem to be hints of the Samuel story; there was something special about this child and, seeing that, they decided that they wouldn't be afraid of the king's edict.

And so, after keeping the child safe for three months . . . by the way, the Jews have a legend which is that, up to three months, a baby could be kept quiet. But what the Egyptians did – again this is a Jewish legend, it's not in the Bible – was, because the Pharaoh was suspicious that the Israelite women were keeping these babies back, they took newborn Egyptian babies into the Israelite homes and deliberately rubbed thorn bushes on their feet and hands to make them cry, because a crying baby makes another sleeping baby wake up and cry. And so, a crying Egyptian baby identified a crying Israelite baby and that baby could be taken out and killed.

Emotional fear

Amram and Jochebed are the heroes here and, despite the king's edict, they say to themselves, 'This child seems to have something we can't quite define and we will therefore not be afraid of the king's edict.' But what does that mean? Are we seriously expected to believe that the threat from a dictator Pharaoh didn't cause this couple any emotional fear at all? That just seems to me wholly out of keeping with human experience. I think what the writer is saying is, 'They may have been afraid emotionally but the fear didn't dictate the decision because of faith.'

The presence of faith in your life doesn't mean you will never feel afraid, it means that you will have the courage to do the right thing despite how you feel. And, interestingly enough, that's illustrated a few verses further down, about faith defeating fear. Verse 27: 'By faith he left Egypt, not fearing the king's anger; he persevered because he saw him who is invisible.'

There's a problem here. There's an exegetical problem, an interpretative problem, and a direct conflict between the Old Testament story in Exodus and this sermon in the book of Hebrews, because Exodus says that Moses was afraid (Exod. 2:14), and Hebrews says he wasn't afraid. What's going on? I think it's precisely what I've just hinted at about the parents.

I believe that Genesis, Exodus, Leviticus, Numbers and Deuteronomy have got massive editorial input from Moses. I think he would have been aware of much of the material – some of it he would have collated, much of it I think he would have contributed to. Given, if it's true, his ability with the alphabet, he may have written significant sections. What I do know is that, if he was writing in the Exodus account, he would have talked about an emotional fear: 'Moses was afraid and ran away.' But the writer to the Hebrews is pointing to another reality. Moses may have been emotionally afraid but he didn't let the fear dictate the activity and so he went away into Midian, was there getting ready for the return he was about to make, and so his faith helped him overcome an emotional fear and not have his actions determined by that fear.

The first point here reminds us that faith defeats fear – not necessarily the emotion of fear, but it defeats the incapacity which the emotion of fear brings, and allows us to make godly decisions. God is not asking us to feel unafraid emotionally, but to act in a way that relies on and trusts in his promises, sometimes despite how we feel.

Faith makes radical choices (vv. 24–26)

Secondly, faith makes radical choices: 'By faith Moses, when he had grown up, refused to be known as the son of Pharaoh's daughter' (v. 24). He had everything going for him: a wealthy upbringing, as much food as he could possibly want, all the luxury of an Egyptian palace upbringing, and then, apparently, Stephen seems to imply in his sermon, around the age of forty (Acts 6:23), he made the decision that he was going to be identified with his own people and, there seems to be an implication (v. 25), with the God of his people. He was going to be identified with them, even though the cost was going to be enormous in purely physical terms and, as it turned out, in all sorts of other terms as well. He refused to enjoy the 'fleeting pleasures of sin' (v. 25, ESV) or, as the King James' Version says, 'the pleasures of sin for a season'. 'He regarded disgrace for the sake of Christ as of greater value than the treasures of Egypt' (v. 26).

In some senses, that's simply anachronistic: Moses couldn't have done something 'for Christ', strictly speaking – he didn't know about him, he was centuries before. But the preacher, using a kind of preaching licence, is helping us understand that Moses, reaching out beyond what he actually knows, wants to love and serve God and embraces – in the same sacrificial way that Christ embraces his own destiny and dies on the cross – his destiny, which is self-sacrifice. He embraces a destiny which involves him saying no to pleasure and no to riches and no to political power and influence and yes to suffering and yes to identifying with the hurting people of God. Faith enables us to make radical choices in terms of discipleship.

Earlier this year, I was in the east of India, in Orissa. I spoke at a conference of several hundred pastors. One of the requirements for being there was that you'd either lost a family member in a recent riot – the autumn of 2008 or the autumn of 2007 – or you'd had your home destroyed. Imagine that, as a requirement for a conference. And, speaking to people, I spoke about forgiveness. At the end, a pastor came to see me. He said, 'Steve, just answer me this,' – it wasn't critical, it wasn't aggressive – 'how can I forgive the man who murdered my father and I see him in the village every day?'

Those Christians were given choices at the time, by some of the Hindu fundamentalists who persecuted them, to abandon Christianity and stay in their homes, or maintain their walk with Christ and be obliterated – or at least, their homes would be destroyed. Thousands of them were moved into refugee camps on India's eastern border. Even then, as recently as a few months ago, the camps were being visited by people who were saying, 'If you'll just renounce your faith, come back, it'll all be fine.' But rather than the security and pleasure and safety of engagement in a culture which they simply couldn't embrace – they chose to live for Jesus Christ. I was deeply humbled by that. I've never had to face that kind of radical choice. An organization called Open Doors are trying to get people to pray for the persecuted church in Orissa. Pray for these folk.

And it's not just people in India, is it? We live in a world of deep decadence. In the twenty-first century, our society is desperate, the credit crunch has shaken much of western confidence to its roots, and yet still we long for success, for luxury, for the conspicuous consumption which characterizes so much of the western world.

The Moses moment

One day, brothers and sisters, we are going to be called to decide: In whose kingdom do we live? By whose values do we walk? To whom do we bow the knee? And, in the end, though it will be tempting to believe we can live under the authority of both kingdoms, there is a call coming, I believe, to the church of Jesus in our nation, a call which will be challenging to our easy western comfortable materialism, and it will shake us to our core. And I think God is calling the church in this country to a radical level of discipleship that says, 'I might have this and that in terms of material possessions but actually, I serve a different King and the King I'm choosing to serve is Jesus Christ. And if that means an absence of material things, if that means I don't buy the "consume and live and own" society, if it means that, then I'm prepared to do it for the sake of Jesus Christ.'

Brothers and sisters, are you ready for the Moses moment? Because I do think that the time will come. It is easy for us to assume we can just drift along with this culture, which isn't threatening yet to kill us or imprison us as in Orissa or as in North Korea or as in vast tracts of the Islamic world; it isn't doing that. It is way more assiduous and way more subtle. We are being lulled to sleep because materialism is not the brutal threat, but it is the assiduous cancer which destroys our will to be radical disciples.

Moses said, 'I'm going to identify with my slave people, if it means doing the right thing.' That's a deep challenge in this Moses material. He could have had everything; he chose to have nothing. And God so blesses him, he becomes an incredible agent of God's victory.

Faith embraces grace (v. 28)

Thirdly, 'By faith' verse 28, 'he kept' – some people think that the Greek here should say 'he instituted the Passover', because, in the Exodus material, it says he told them to put blood on the doorposts and so on and then he told them to keep on doing it year in year out, as a memory of what happened (Exod. 12:1–28).

What were they asked to do? They were asked to paint blood on the outside of the doorposts and then to believe that the angel of death would pass over. You can hear the Israelites talking to Moses: 'Is that it? Should we kind of put up a big net, keep the angel away? Should we guard the house all night?' 'No,' he says to them, 'no, that's right. Kill a lamb.' And this resonates with the sermon which is Hebrews, which is about the sacrifice which is Christ, who ultimately becomes the Paschal – the Passover lamb – on our behalf. And so, faith embraces grace.

Nothing but the blood

What is it that guarantees our home in heaven? Nothing but the blood of Jesus. What is it that gets our sins forgiven? What is it that grants that I'm going to be accepted? Is it because I'm clever? No. Is it because I'm a Baptist? We can rule that out. Why is it? Is it because I'm a speaker at the Keswick Convention? Is there a special place in heaven for the Keswick Convention committee? Nothing but the blood of Jesus. What can wash away my sin? Nothing but the blood of Jesus.

Whoever you are, what are you counting on to get into God's heaven and into his kingdom? I pray, like Moses, you're going to count on the blood of the Lamb. This time, not a lamb from flocks in the land of Goshen but the Lamb of God who, John tells us, came to take away the sin of the world (John 1:29). Trust in that sacrifice, because that is the only hope for all of us.

The final word (v. 29)

Fourthly, the last verse of this section, we have Moses here – what's he doing? He's with the people of God. 'By faith the people passed through the Red Sea as on dry land; but when the Egyptians tried to do so, they were drowned' (v. 29). They escaped on dry ground. How did they escape? Was it because an east wind blew all night, as Exodus tells us (Exod. 14:21)? Absolutely. But was it because God worked a miracle? Absolutely.

The Red Sea story tells us not that whenever we pray in faith, God will grant us a miracle – it doesn't teach us that. It teaches us that God always has the final word. He'd promised the children of Israel deliverance. He told it to Moses and Aaron, they're there announcing it and they come up against Pharaoh who says, 'I don't care what God says, you're not going.' And so they say, 'There's going to be a load of bad times come upon you, ten lots of bad times.' And he says, 'I don't care, you're not going.' After a few, he says, 'You can go.' Then he changes his mind. Then, after the death of the first-born, he's shattered and so he lets them go and even then, he decides to thwart the will of almighty God – he sends the whole army out after them. God says, 'Enough, I've said these people will go free and I have the last word, and so my promise will be fulfilled.' The Red Sea parts, the people walk across and they are free, why? Because God always grants a miracle? No, but because God always has the last word. His promise is true. He's in charge.

Brothers and sisters, rise to that excitement! God has the last word in our lives. Do you feel broken and hurt and defeated? God's promise of this eternal security in heaven with his Son, an eternity of celebration. That's the final word, not your current circumstances, not the fears and the doubts you currently feel.

I've read to the end of this book, we win. His is the final word. For all of you facing huge issues: by faith, God will have the final word. I don't know whether he's going to heal your body or not, whether he's going to massively change your circumstances or not, please God he will. But, whatever he does, the final word of history, the final word in your life and mine, our destiny resides not in the hand of a capricious government – whatever laws it may pass – not in the hands of some philosopher, not in the hands of our own moods and the insecurities of our own circumstances, but our future lies in the hands of the God who has the last word.

An art gallery, a painting, a picture of a chessboard, the word 'checkmate' written underneath and a desperately sad-looking Christian, and the devil with horns on the other side, gloating that the Christian is checkmated. For months, the exhibition continues, until a chess grand master appears in the gallery and, finding himself at the picture, stares at it intently. Suddenly, with wide-eyed surprise, he shouts, 'No, get the artist back. The king has a move to make yet.' It's never checkmate for the devil, the King has another move to make yet. He has another move in our culture, another move in our churches, another move in my life and another move in yours. I want to tell you tonight God has the final word. Amen!

A woman finds faith – Rahab

by Peter Maiden

Peter Maiden

Peter Maiden stepped down from being Keswick Ministries' Chairman in 2009, but continues to serve as a Trustee and member of the Convention Council. He is also the International Director of Operation Mobilization, and travels extensively to fulfil his commitment to them and their staff, spread over 116 countries. Peter also serves on the board of a number of other Christian groups, is an Elder of Hebron Evangelical Church in Carlisle, and an Honorary Canon of Carlisle Cathedral. Peter enjoys family life with his wife, Win, and their three grown-up children and seven grandchildren. His book, *Discipleship*, was the first to be published in the Keswick Foundations series.

A woman finds faith – Rahab: Hebrews 11:31

Let me explain what we're seeking to do at this Convention. We're talking about faith that works and, particularly in the evenings, we're looking at great characters who displayed faith in their lives. We find them all in the eleventh chapter of Hebrews, from which we've just read, and tonight we're looking at a lady: Rahab. She's a very fascinating lady.

James Montgomery Boyce likens Rahab to the fourth-century Christian hero Athanasius. He was born about AD295 in Alexandria, Egypt, and died in 373. He certainly didn't have an easy life. He lived through the great Trinitarian controversies and, for much of his life, Athanasius was almost the sole defender of what we would today recognize as orthodox Christianity. Athanasius defended the deity of Jesus Christ. He recognized that our salvation depended upon that truth. Emperors denounced him; they frequently sent him into exile. He was actually exiled from his bishopric five times. The church turned against him and, on one occasion, the story goes, someone came to him and said, 'Athanasius, the whole world is against you.' And his reply was, 'Then is Athanasius against the world.' Talk about standing against the tide.

This is the story of Rahab, standing against the world of Canaan, making lonely and incredibly courageous decisions, which could well have cost her her life, and doing so because, somehow, she had learned about God and trusted in him.

I appreciate I may be speaking to many who find themselves in a lonely place. Maybe in your home, your school, your university, your place of work, you are in a minority as a believer and may feel the whole world is against you. Courageous decisions are called for constantly in your Christian life, and loneliness may well be a regular experience for you. It's been my prayer throughout this day, as I've been looking again at this passage, that you might be encouraged tonight by the example of Rahab.

Rahab's decision for God

We're going to look at her life in three very easy ways. Let's look at her situation for a moment. She was a Gentile, and Gentiles, as Paul explained to the Ephesians, were excluded from citizenship in Israel. So she was a foreigner to the covenants of the promise; without hope because she was without God in the world. She wasn't just a Gentile, she was an Amorite and, among the many peoples of the land of Canaan, they are singled out. They seem to take evil to new extremes, even sacrificing children as part of their depraved religious practices. She was also a prostitute. Some commentators say the word translated 'prostitute' could be translated 'innkeeper' but the majority of commentators conclude that she was a practising prostitute. She's living in the city of Jericho, it's a walled, fortified city and, as the threat from the Israelites becomes clearer and clearer, Jericho is ever more heavily defended. Chapter 6 of Joshua, the first verse, describes the city as 'tightly shut up'.

Rahab has a huge decision to make. 'Am I going to put my trust in this city with its king, its army, its fortifications, or am I going to put my trust in this God that I've heard of? As I look around and listen to the conversation of the city, I can see which way people are going. It seems to be unanimous. "This city," they say, "is our hope. Surely sticking together, in this city, is our best hope of survival."'

Jericho, of course, was what Rahab knew. Its people and their practices were what she was familiar with. Who was this God she was beginning to hear about? What would it mean to trust him, to pin her future on him, to throw in her lot with the people of God rather than her own people? John talked about Abraham on Monday and spoke of a faith which was willing to leave Ur of the Chaldeans, to leave all that Abraham knew and was familiar with. Rahab faces a very similar challenge. Decisions such as these have been called for throughout history and they're still called for today. Will we trust in the apparent strength of man and his institutions, or will we trust in God? Do we retreat into the apparent security of what we know, or do we step out for God?

Psalm 20

This psalm, it seems, was a sort of pledge of loyalty, used before a military campaign. Derek Kidner describes it in this way, 'The shape of the psalm brings the scene before us as the king prepares to march and his men are grouped with their standards.' Look at that image in your mind: the king is there, the people are around him with their standards and they're prepared to march. That's the scene for this psalm.

The first five verses, it seems, are spoken by the massed armies, spoken to the king

> May the LORD answer you when you are in distress;
> may the name of the God of Jacob protect you.
> May he send you help from the sanctuary
> and grant you support from Zion.
> May he remember all your sacrifices
> and accept your burnt offerings.
> May he give you the desire of your heart
> and make all your plans succeed.
> We will shout for joy when you are victorious
> and will lift up our banners in the name of our God.
> May the LORD grant all your requests (Ps. 20:1–5).

And then a single voice is heard, probably the voice of the king himself

> Now I know that the LORD saves his anointed;
> he answers him from his holy heaven

with the saving power of his right hand.
Some trust in chariots and some in horses,
but we trust in the name of the LORD our God.
They are brought to their knees and fall,
but we rise up and stand firm (Ps. 20: 6–8).

Then all the people are heard again

O LORD, save the king! Answer us when we call! (v. 9)

As I read it, the hairs on the back of my neck almost rise. It is a stir-ring example of first a people and then their king pledging to trust in God alone: not in their chariots, not in their horses but in the name of the Lord their God. So which way will Rahab go, the city or the God of Israel? Will she trust her people, their familiar culture and practices, or will she step out into the largely unknown and certainly untried?

You may know that in Operation Mobilization, we've just laun-ched a ship, *Logos Hope*. I'll never forget the early meetings when we were discussing that project. We knew that it was a project of a dimen-sion we'd never considered before. It would take us into areas of trust-ing God, as individuals and as a movement, that we'd never even con-sidered before. I can remember how doubtful we were. We went back and forward: should we move into areas which were really unknown to us or should we stay with what we felt we could handle, what we felt we could manage? I can remember the fear and the expectation rising as we sensed God pushing us towards that project.

How much did Rahab know about God? Remember she had no Bible, she'd heard no preaching, she'd never been to a Convention – but she had heard stories.

We have heard how the LORD dried up the water of the Red Sea for you when you came out of Egypt, and what you did to Sihon and Og, the two kings of the Amorites east of the Jordan, whom you com-pletely destroyed. When we heard of it, our hearts melted and every-one's courage failed because of you, for the LORD your God is God in heaven above and on the earth below (Josh. 2:10,11).

Quite simply, this lady had heard stories and those stories must have had particular significance for her. When God sent the Israelites to take on Zion, this was his promise: 'This very day I will begin to put the terror and fear of you on all the nations under heaven' (Deut. 2:25). What did Rahab say to the spies? 'When we heard of it, our hearts sank and everyone's courage failed because of you' (Josh. 2:11). This was a calculated, strategic display of the majesty of the God of Israel. And Rahab had heard about it. When they defeated Og, they took all his cities, sixty of them according to Deuteronomy chapter 3. They were all fortified and had high walls with gates and bars and, one after another, sixty of those cities had fallen. Rahab had heard what God had done and she believed in him as a result. It's amazing that many in Israel had not only heard what God had done, they'd also seen his acts with their own eyes, but they were known for their unbelief and their murmurings. This is a quite remarkable act of faith from the most unlikely of women.

I don't want to get into too much speculation, but I wonder how she'd heard these stories. Was it from her customers, so to speak? 'Did you hear what happened to Og and to Zion? Those fortified cities, they didn't stand for long, did they? Sixty of them went down, one after another, not much hope for Jericho.' What we possibly have here is an immoral pagan woman who, quite possibly, even as she's going about her business of prostitution, hears about the true God of Israel. She begins to think, 'This is no local god typical of the Canaanite gods, this is the one God in heaven above and on the earth below.' And she makes her great decision to trust in him.

As one commentator says, 'As long as that can happen and it does happen, we can never despair about anybody and we never need to despair about ourselves.' Is there anyone you're despairing about? You've been praying for them for years? There are people in my life like this. The story of Rahab is an amazing testimony of the truth that no one is beyond the reach of the mercy of God.

Rahab's deliverance by God

Can we take this truth about the mercy of God one step further? Why did God send his servants into Jericho before its destruction? Some say it wasn't God who sent them; it was Joshua and it was a sign of his unbelief. God had already told Joshua, the critics say, that this city would be destroyed, so why did he need to send spies? But I hope you don't live like that. God has also promised us victory but I hope you're not sitting in your spiritual easy chair, waiting for it to happen, leaving it all somehow to God. He expects us to prepare for battle, even when the victory is assured.

I don't think these spies went just to send back information. They probably didn't realize it but they were God's servants, sent for the salvation of Rahab and her family. God had been working in Rahab's heart. True faith in him, as she heard of his works, was being birthed, and now God sends his messengers to Jericho to confirm her faith and physically save her. Joshua is a book full of conflicts. The sin of the Amorites has reached its full measure, the people were ripe for judgement, but the first story in the book is a story of wonderful mercy, shown by God to a most unlikely individual. And God's merciful intervention could not be clearer. How will God show his mercy? When the armies go in, will they somehow surround the house where the scarlet cord hangs in the window and make sure that house is not attacked? Rahab's house was on the wall. It seems everything came tumbling down but Rahab's house. Verse 22 of Joshua 6 puts it like this: 'Joshua said to the two men who had spied out the land, "Go into the prostitute's house and bring her out and all who belong to her, in accordance with your oath to her."'

A note in the Archaeological Study Bible informs us that German excavations on the northern section of the Jericho site, between 1907 and 1909, uncovered a portion of the lower city wall that did not fall as it did everywhere else: 'A still standing section rose as high as 2.5 metres with houses built against it still intact. A second wall at the crest of the embankment revealed that these particular houses were situated between the upper and lower city walls and were thus in the city wall.'

This is the amazing merciful intervention of God, towards one Gentile Amorite woman with an immoral history, who has trusted in him. But as we follow Rahab's story, we see that this stream of mercy towards her doesn't stop there. There's much more to it. You might imagine that, with her heritage and her background, the best she could hope for was a sort of second-class existence among God's people. Something like the Gibeonites, who were allowed to live among the Jews as woodcutters and water-carriers for the community. But not at all. Rahab marries a Jew, and their son is Boaz who marries Ruth, the Moabitess; their son is Obed who was the father of Jesse, who was the father of King David. So this Gentile Amorite prostitute becomes an ancestor of our Lord Jesus Christ. Someone used or abused by men, no doubt someone who struggled with her self-worth and her identity, has her whole life transformed by the mercy of God.

I've got a letter here from one of our pastors in north India, telling me about a Dalit brother called Eliphaz. Eliphaz was born a Dalit in a village in northern India. The Dalits are the untouchables, the lowest of the low in that society. But he wasn't only born a Dalit, he was born a crippled Dalit. This is his story.

> I was a laughing stock before everyone. I didn't have good looks. I limped my way through the village. People talked about me in hushed tones. I was used to strange glances. Everyone was above me. I had no equal. I was the odd one. I came to regard myself as less than human. My future seemed bleak. There was nothing to look forward to. I limped my way to the village school without dignity or honour. I was destined to perish like an unattended plant.

And then a little church is established in the village. He hears song, the song draws him to the church. He finds Christ. Through the pastor, he's introduced to an OM team. 'And miraculously' he says,

> one day, I became part of a team in Andhra Pradesh. As someone who'd grown up without self-esteem, I struggled initially. The oneness, the

equality I observed in that team, startled me. Equal treatment and brotherhood, it was a revelation; cross-cultural exposure was breathtaking. Gradually, I began to learn English and soon I found myself preaching in English. To my astonishment, people were listening to me. All my life, I'd lived with this disgusting inferiority.

He goes on to talk about how he gets some training at a theological college in India, and he was sent into a new village where there were no Christians and he was the evangelist. And today there are 100 Dalit believers in that village. Then he tells this story of the 26 January this year.

The Hindu village was gearing up for Republic Day. I looked out of my window. I saw the headmaster of the school and a few teachers approaching my home. They told me, 'There's a very special occasion in the school on Republic Day and we're inviting four dignitaries, including a senior government official.' And after a pause, to my total astonishment, they said, 'Pastor, we request you to be the fourth dignitary.' Lightning flashed through my head. 'I, destined to perish like an unattended plant: through Christ, I have value; I have worth; my life totally transformed.

Tragically, it's not just Dalits who are abused. I appreciate I'll be speaking to a large number in this tent who have suffered, or are suffering, abuse. It might be within the family; it might be workplace abuse; it might even, tragically, be within the church. Insecure leaders, whose identity is not in Christ but more in their job or in their title, often, without realizing it, to defend their position, become abusive leaders. You may be a casualty of that this evening. Rahab's testimony is that faith in God can make you whole. It may be a long journey to wholeness but you can start that journey. You can walk the road which Eliphaz travelled: it may be a long road but you can start that journey. This is the picture I want to fix in your mind: of a Gentile Amorite prostitute, who is now an ancestor of our Lord Jesus Christ. It's a picture of the mercy of God, mercy which can reach into the darkest, most hopeless corner of our lives.

Rahab's usefulness in the service of God

As a prostitute, living on the wall of Jericho, Rahab could never have imagined in her wildest dreams that we would be talking about her today, speaking of how she came to play a key role in the purposes of God and, indeed, in the salvation which we enjoy. But, one day, God's mission came knocking at Rahab's door and she was available. Her willingness to be available involved great courage and great faith. It is interesting that, at this point of opportunity, her past life does not disqualify her. She does the right thing at this time and God takes her up and uses her.

When we think of serving the purposes of God, I can guarantee that there will be at least two responses. 'What have I to offer?' is one. Others may well respond, 'I've blown it big time and I can never be useful again.' I get so angry. You might not consider me to be an angry person, but I get so angry at the success of Satan from keeping so much gifting, so much experience, in God's people unused and undeveloped. The story of Rahab testifies to the fact that no one is beyond the mercy of God, but it also testifies to the fact that God uses the most unlikely of people to serve his purposes. In the second chapter of James, the apostle is writing about true faith that always results in works and he gives just two examples. One is Abraham, the father of the faithful, who was ready to sacrifice his own son if God called for that. It is no surprise that James should use him as an example. But his second example is Rahab. Here, in Hebrews 11, only two women are mentioned as an example of faith from the Old Testament. And once again Rahab is one of the two.

My time has gone but I don't think I can afford to finish without mentioning the scarlet cord. When the spies agreed that Rahab would be saved the destruction coming on the city, they made this demand of her: 'This oath you made us swear will not be binding on us unless, when we enter the land, you have tied this scarlet cord in the window' (Josh. 2:17,18). Commentators tell us that there's a tradition in the church, going all the way back to Clement of Rome and even before that, that the scarlet cord represents the blood of Christ. Some see this cord running all through the Bible from Abel's sacrifice to

Calvary. I don't know if Rahab's cord specifically represented the blood of Christ, although there is a great similarity between this and the blood on the lintels and doorposts of the houses of the Israelites in Egypt. But I do know the only reason I can stand here as a child of God, like Rahab, is the blood of Christ. The only reason I can offer anything in the service of Christ, is the power of his blood.

I get increasingly frustrated at the successes of Satan. God can take a Rahab and restore her dignity completely and make her thoroughly useful in his purposes. God can do that. But still I think of a lady in my church who struggles to ever come to the communion table because of past stuff in her life. She knows, intellectually, the blood of Christ has dealt with it, but Satan still uses that past rotten stuff to rob her of her joy and to rob her of much Christian usefulness. The story of Rahab is of a God who can take a Gentile Amorite prostitute and make her an ancestor of his Son. Don't allow any more robbery from the enemy. Let's hang that scarlet cord and put our faith completely in the finished work of Christ.

Endnotes

The challenge of living in a fallen world

1 Cited in Charles Colson, *Against the Night* (Ann Arbor: Vine Books, 1989).
2 Iain Murray, *David Martyn Lloyd-Jones, The Fight of Faith 1939–1981* (Edinburgh: Banner of Truth Trust, 1990).
3 Robert Massie, *Peter the Great* (New York: Ballantine Books Inc., 1997).
Godliness from head to toe

Godliness from head to toe: James 2

1 Walter Kaiser, *What Does the Lord Require?* (Baker Academic, 2009), p.36.
2 Michael Townsend, *The Epistle of James* (Epworth, 1994), p.34.
3 Solomon Andria, *The Africa Bible Commentary* (San Francisco: Word Alive and Zondervan, 2006), p.1512.
4 Ronald Sider, *Rich Christians in an Age of Hunger* (London: Hodder & Stoughton, 1976).
5 Sam Harris, *Letter to a Christian Nation* (Bantam, 2007).
6 Craig Blomberg and Marian Karnell, *Exegetical Commentary on the New Testament: James* (Zondervan: 2008), p.135.
7 *The Times*, 16 September, 2008.
8 Martin Luther King, *Strength to Live* (Fontana, 1969), p.37.
9 Quoted in Timothy Dudley-Smith, *Authentic Christianity: From the Writings of John Stott* (Nottingham: IVP, 1995), p.175.
10 Quoted in Blomberg and Karnell, p.139.

Abraham, the father of faith

[1] William L. Lane, *Word Biblical Commentary: Hebrews 9-13* (Nashville: Thomas Nelson, 2001).

Keswick 2009

Keswick Convention 2009 teaching is available now.
All talks recorded at Keswick 2009, including Bible Readings by
Dale Ralph Davis, Jonathan Lamb and Vaughan Roberts, are
available now on CD, MP3 download and DVD★ from
www.essentialchristian.com/keswick

Keswick teaching is now available on MP3 download.
Just select the MP3 option on the teaching you want, and after
paying at the checkout your computer will receive the teaching
MP3 download. Now you can listen to teaching on the go; on your
iPod, PDA or even your mobile phone.

Over fifty years of Keswick teaching all in one place.

Visit www.essentialchristian.com/keswick to browse Keswick
Convention Bible teaching from as far back as 1952! You can also
browse albums by worship leaders and artistes who have performed
at Keswick, including Stuart Townend, Phatfish and Keith and
Kristyn Getty, plus Keswick Live albums and the *Precious Moments*
collection of DVDs.

To order, visit www.essentialchristian.com/keswick or call
0845 607 1672

★Not all talks available on DVD.

KESWICK MINISTRIES

Keswick Ministries is committed to the deepening of the spiritual life in individuals and church communities through the careful exposition and application of Scripture, seeking to encourage the following:

Lordship of Christ – To encourage submission to the Lordship of Christ in personal and corporate living
Life Transformation – To encourage a dependency upon the indwelling and fullness of the Holy Spirit for life transformation and effective living
Evangelism and Mission – To provoke a strong commitment to the breadth of evangelism and mission in the British Isles and worldwide
Discipleship – To stimulate the discipling and training of people of all ages in godliness, service and sacrificial living
Unity – To provide a practical demonstration of evangelical unity

Keswick Ministries is committed to achieving its aims by:

• providing Bible-based training courses for youth workers and young people (via Root 66) and Bible Weeks for Christians of all backgrounds who want to develop their skills and learn more
• promoting the use of books, DVDs and CDs so that Keswick's teaching ministry is brought to a wider audience at home and abroad
• producing TV and radio programmes so that superb Bible talks can be broadcast to you at home
• publishing up-to-date details of Keswick's exciting news and events on our website so that you can access material and purchase Keswick products online
• publicizing Bible teaching events in the UK and overseas so that Christians of all ages are encouraged to attend 'Keswick' meetings closer to home and grow in their faith
• putting the residential accommodation of the Convention Centre at the disposal of churches, youth groups, Christian organizations and many others, at very reasonable rates, for holidays and outdoor activities in a stunning location

If you'd like more details please look at our website (www.keswickministries.org) or contact the Keswick Ministries office by post, email or telephone as given below.

**Keswick Ministries, Convention Centre, Skiddaw Street,
Keswick, Cumbria, CA12 4BY
Tel: 017687 80075; Fax 017687 75276;
email: info@keswickministries.org**

Keswick 2010

Week 1: 17th– 23rd July
Week 2: 24th–30th July
Week 3: 31st July–6th August

The annual Keswick Convention takes place in the heart of the English Lake District, an area of outstanding national beauty. It offers an unparalled opportunity to listen to gifted Bible exposition, meet Christians from all over the world and enjoy the grandeur of God's creation. Each of the three weeks has a series of morning Bible readings, and then a varied programme of seminars, lectures, book cafés, prayer meetings, concerts, drama and other events throughout the day, with evening meetings that combine worship and teaching. There is also a full programme for children and young people, and a special track for those with learning difficulties which takes place in week 2. K2, the interactive track for those in their twenties and thirties, also takes place in week 2.

The theme for Keswick 2010 is *Christ-Centred Renewal*
The Bible readings will be given by:
Don Carson (week 1) on Matthew
Paul Mallard (week 2) on Revelation 2 and 3
Alistair Begg (week 3) on Romans 8

Other confirmed speakers are Steve Brady, Derek Burnside, Simon Downham, Dave Fenton, Liam Goligher, Jonathan Lamb, Peter Maiden, Jeremy McQuoid, Hugh Palmer, Jonathan Stephen, Joe Stowell, Terry Virgo and Wendy Virgo.